Sensible
Stimulation

Sensible Stimulation

The key to your child's
development during
the first three years
of life

Marga Grey

Published by Metz Press
1 Cameronians Avenue
Welgemoed, 7530 South Africa

First published in 2009
Copyright © Metz Press 2015
Text copyright © Marga Grey

All rights reserved. No part of this publication may be reproduced, stored in a retrieval system or transmitted in any form or by any means, electronic, mechanical, photocopying, recording or otherwise, without the prior written permission of the copyright owners.

Publisher	Wilsia Metz
Translation	Louise Vorster
Proofreader	Deborah Morbin
Design & layout	Liezl Maree
Illustrations	Nikki Miles

ISBN 978-1-920268-13-8

Contents

Introduction 9

Chapter 1:	Getting ready for parenthood	11
Chapter 2:	The learning process according to your child's potential	15
	Potential	16
	The learning process	18
	Stimulation	20
Chapter 3:	The stimulating environment	23
	Genes versus environment	23
	How does stimulation take place?	25
	A stimulating environment	26
	Your relationship with your child	27
	The choice of play	29
	Toys	31
Chapter 4:	Brain development	39
	The development of the nervous system	39
	Brain growth	40
	Nerve myelinisation	41
	Active brain areas	42
	Critical periods for stimulation	42
	The development of the embryo and foetus during the first semester of pregnancy	42
	Prenatal influences on the brain	45
	Guidelines for promoting normal development	47
Chapter 5:	Sensory development	49
	Sense of touch	51
	Vestibular sense	55
	Sense of smell	59
	Sense of taste	60
	Sense of vision	61
	Sense of hearing	65

Chapter 6:	Motor development 69
	Acquiring motor skills 71
	The importance of motor skills 72
	Stimulating motor development 73
	balance 73
	bilateral integration and lateralisation 76
	motor planning 77
	gross motor movements 78
	fine motor movements 79
Chapter 7:	Body image 81
Chapter 8:	Self-image 87
	Happiness 89
	Fostering a healthy self-image 91
	Preventing a low self-image 94
	The role of the environment 95
Chapter 9:	The development of play 97
	Stages of play 97
	Aspects that influence play 101
Chapter 10:	Speech and language development 103
	Pre-speech communication 104
	Vocabulary 106
	Promotion of language and listening skills 107
Chapter 11:	Perceptual and cognitive development 109
	Perceptual development 109
	Cognitive development 112
	creativity 112
	conceptual ability 115
	moral values 118
Chapter 12:	Emotions 121
	Emotional intelligence 122
	Emotional development 123
	Social adaptation 125
	The child's perception of emotions 126

Chapter 13: Parenthood 131
    Parental types 131
    Emotional coaching...134
    The effects of emotional coaching 135
    The father's role..136
Chapter 14: Discipline 137
    The importance of discipline 138
    Punishment...139
    Routine... 140
    Obedience 141
    Honesty...142
Chapter 15: Problem solving and conflict...143
    Solving problems 143
    Dealing with conflict 145

Conclusion 147
Appendix 1 148
Appendix 2 157
Additional reading 160

Whatever pronoun is used refers equally to baby boys and girls, mothers and fathers, and male and female caregivers. One form has been used simply to avoid the clumsy use of he/she or him/her and so on.

Introduction

Parenthood is a new phase of life which you are likely to enter with great excitement and anticipation, determined to make a roaring success of it. That is why you prepare yourself, read up, attend workshops, seek advice, listen to friends who already have children, and decide how you are going to approach being a parent, being a mom or a dad, and implement it successfully. However, soon after their baby's birth, most parents discover that nothing could really prepare them for all the demands that have now become part of their daily routine. They come to realise that the life they now have is radically different from the one they had before they became parents. It is a life that you can only experience when you are a parent yourself.

This book aims to inform, guide and support parents by giving them more insight into their child's early development. Through knowledge and understanding, parents can guide their children, helping them to become balanced adults and confident members of society.

In order to fully understand your child, you need a knowledge of the development of the total child, as well as of the processes every person goes through while developing from babyhood to childhood to adulthood. Raising children has so many facets that it requires a proper study and a whole series of books to gather all the information. To buy a booklet on improving your child's self-image, for instance, when you notice that something is wrong, is like putting a new ball on the court at half-time and thinking that it will swing the game in favour of the losing team. There is much more involved than the quality of the ball.

So, this book is not about one aspect of parenthood, but rather an attempt to touch upon most aspects of parenthood and child rearing, explaining to the parent what goes on inside the child. Once a parent understands this, many of the educational principles will happen automatically and the parent will stimulate and educate the child without constantly having to consult a text book. The first three years of a child's life are the most significant, as they are fundamental to all further development. This book focuses on the development during those early years. Each aspect is explained as practically and simply as possible, with games that you can participate in with your child. Consult the reading list on page 160 if you need more information on any specific topic.

For the sake of order, different aspects of development are discussed in different chapters. However, all aspects of childhood and humanhood are so narrowly intertwined that no single chapter can stand apart from the rest of the book. Everything must be seen in the right context, as part of the whole. Although the book focuses on the first three years, many of the educational principles can be applied throughout your child's growing years.

No ages are linked to the various development stages, as that could create expectations in parents, followed by needless anxiety when those expectations are not realised. In my opinion, it is more important that children go through each stage in their own time rather than reaching a certain stage at a certain age. As will be seen later, all babies and children go through the same successive stages of development (e.g. sitting, crawling, walking), and it is more important to go through all three stages than to be able to walk by a certain age.

If a child does have a significant lag that could indicate a neurological problem or syndrome, it will be spotted and attended to when the child is taken for his routine medical checkups. It is more important to know, enjoy, and spend time with your child than to pressurize him to master certain tasks at certain ages. Likewise, the games in this book that you can play with your child are not age-related. The degree of difficulty for each game can be adapted by the parent to match the child's abilities, rather than his age.

The book starts off with a discussion on potential and guidelines for a stimulating environment, followed by one aspect of the child's development in each successive chapter. This does not mean, however, that any aspect or ability can develop independently from any other aspect; all aspects develop simultaneously, are equally important and have an effect on every other aspect.

1
Getting ready for parenthood

Parenthood goes much further than just your child or children. It involves all your child's friends, as well as every person who contributes to his education and every person who thinks that he or she has a right to advise you and/or your child in any way. It also involves your team mate – the child's other parent – and the extended family whose support can be invaluable, but who may sometimes fail to lend that much-needed support.

Maybe it would be easier to raise and educate a child all by yourself, exactly the way you deemed good and right, with no-one else influencing or judging anything you did. However, this would mean withdrawing to an island and isolating yourself and your child from the rest of the world. Your child would function well, precisely according to your standards, but probably nowhere else other than on the island. Because we are social creatures, however, we must raise our children to function within the social group. Just as a good coach coaches a winning team by working on many different aspects, a good parent works on many different facets of the child, as well as on the environment that can influence the child. Just as the good coach always has his ear on the ground to listen, look and observe every aspect of his team and his players, a good parent will also observe his or her child – as an individual, but also as a member of the immediate and extended family, and the community to which the child belongs.

In order to fully understand your child, I strongly recommend seeking professional advice. It is extremely difficult for parents to be objective about their own child, about themselves and about the child's other parent. A professional person will be in a far better position to get to the root of a problem and offer practical advice – a hard thing for a subjective parent or family member to do.

A good team leader or coach knows the abilities of each player and employs them in the best possible way. The same goes for parents: You can only guide your children in the right direction if you know their abilities. Children's abilities are directly linked with their level of development. That means a knowledge of child development is required before your player and team can be properly coached. You can seek others' advice, but the parent remains the responsible person and should remain the coach throughout the child's education.

Nowadays most pregnancies are planned to fit in with the parents' ages and careers, as well as with the relationship between the parents. Nevertheless, unplanned pregnancies do occur. The child has not asked for this – therefore both parents have a responsibility to reflect and decide together on how they can raise the child in the best possible way.

Raising a child is a monumental task for which one should be prepared. Preparation begins with the way that you were raised, the expectations that your parents had of you and the rules that your parents expected you to observe. Any parent's automatic response is to teach his or her child the same game that he or she learned to play. Even if you decide that you do not agree with the methods of education that your parents used, and that you want to teach your children different rules and values, your will be inclined to follow the same methods that your parents did.

No doubt your parents did their best in the circumstances and with the knowledge that they possessed. Therefore, you should not analyse your *parents*, but rather their *methods* of education. Also observe the people around you. How were those who are the kind of people that you would like your children to grow up into, brought up? Talk to them, exchange information, broaden your knowledge. Also observe the methods used by parents of smart children. Look at friends and family who have children. Look at children who are happy and content and have a healthy self-image. What do their parents do in comparison to the parents of children who are constantly wailing, crying, nagging and, possibly, also sickly? Talk to the parents, ask them about their household routine, the rules that they have laid down, the game that they play to ensure that they have a winning team.

Have regular and serious talks with your colleague, your partner, your fellow coach in the parenting game – that is your husband, your wife or your partner with whom you want to raise a child. Talk about the different ways in which parents communicate with, and discipline their children, and the routine other people follow in their households. Decide which methods you like, which ones have a positive feel about them and which ones you would like to include in your own parenting game. Also discuss the negative aspects, because if you are simply going to dismiss them as something that you will never do anyway, I can guarantee you that that is exactly what you *will* do!

Analyse the negative aspects of your own educations and discuss the reasons behind them. Parents often come to the shocking realisation that they are reacting in the exact same way that they despise in their own parents or in other people. If you do not deliberately resolve the negative aspects from your own childhood, your automatic response will probably be to act in the same negative manner as your educators. You can even sit down with your partner and make a list of the rules that you want to implement and those that you want to avoid. Do keep in mind, however, that the rules of the parenting game are rather flexible and that they will often have to be adapted according to circumstances or according to a particular child. There is no such thing as a 'text-book baby' or a 'text-book parent'. If you want to be a successful parent, adaptability is the name of the game.

If one, or both of you, discover that there are a considerable number of contradictions in the way that you were raised and the way that you want to raise your children, or in the two parents' expectations and rules for parenting, it is time to consult an expert. If possible difficulties can be solved before the baby is born, it will just make things so much easier. After the baby's birth, you may both feel tired as adaptation to your new routine and your new life can leave you with little time and energy. If you seek professional advice before the baby is born, you will be armed with the name and telephone number of a person whom you know, who knows your story and can give you good advice, even over the telephone. So, a visit before your baby's birth can save you a lot of time and effort later.

A professional person may be a psychologist or a social worker who has sufficient experience in parent guidance, child education and child development. Sometimes people in other disciplines offer a similar service – these include pastors, pastoral psychologists and occupational therapists. Find a reputable person who can be reached easily, so that you will not have trouble getting hold of him or her when you are desperate for help.

In order to be an adaptable parent who acts in your child's best interest, it is important to understand your child. A knowledge of the various levels and stages of development will give you more insight, enabling you to choose the best responses to your child's behaviour. You will know when to be flexible and when to be strict, when to support and when to admonish. You will also know how to stimulate your child, promoting healthy, normal development.

2
The learning process according to your child's potential

In recent decades, much emphasis has been put on the child's pre-school development, and particularly on the year before he starts formal schooling (Grade 1). However, the money and time spent during this year in order to prepare a child for formal schooling, have little value if preparation does not begin in the baby years. In order to become a balanced, successful adult, every human being needs to master certain skills, namely:
- learning to walk
- learning to eat solid foods
- learning to talk
- learning to control body waste (i.e. using the toilet efficiently)
- learning to discern between the genders and control your interest in the differences
- learning to control the basic emotions and be psychologically stable
- learning to conceive of social and physical aspects of the environment and community
- learning to compare yourself emotionally with your parents, family members and other people and to build relationships with various other people (i.e. making and keeping friends)
- learning to differentiate between right and wrong in order to develop a conscience

Careful rereading of this list will help you realise that all these skills start developing in the baby years, and that by the child's third birthday most of them have reached a fair level of advancement. Although these skills improve after the age of three, the basic development happens earlier. This means that the first three years are the most important period of a person's life – this is when the brain, thinking patterns and skills are established.

The foundation of all the abilities that a person will possess later in his life, is laid in his first three years. Therefore the school or teacher cannot always be blamed when a child fails to meet the expectations – instead, it can often be traced back to neglect or a lack of proper stimulation during the child's first three years.

A child learns more in his first three years than for many years to come. Young children are all too often left in the care of an unqualified person, because 'he is still young and does not understand anyway'. The child may not be able to talk and tell you what is going on, but if he is not adequately stimulated, his development will be restricted and inhibited. That brings me to the potential that is inherent in both children and adults.

Potential

All children and adults possess numerous abilities that have never been developed. We do not utilise even a significant portion of our potential. The human brain is made up of millions of cells and connections between those cells, making the brain a more intricate structure than the most advanced computer in the world (which was, after all, conceptualised and designed by the human brain!). We are, however, inclined to underestimate ourselves and our abilities. Every person's brain contains a minimum of one billion (10^{12}) individual neurons or nerve cells, each of which has the ability to connect with between one and 100 000 other neurons. This is a vast number of possible connections. If the brain's ability to form patterns and/or connections had to be expressed in normal handwriting, the row of numbers would cover more than 10,5 million kilometers[1]. With this number of possibilities, the brain can be compared to a keyboard on which 100 million different tunes (behaviour or intelligence types) can be played.

This provides conclusive proof that the potential of the human brain is almost unlimited. Its potential is not determined by the number of neurons (brain cells), but by the number of dendrites (branches) that can grow from each neuron (see figure 1). The increase in the number of dendrites is not age-bound, which means that, contrary to some people's view, the human brain cannot at any stage be fully developed. Further development does, however, happen faster and more efficiently after the basic development has taken place. An eight-year-old who acquired the basic language skills at the critical period for this particular skill, will, for instance, find it easy to extend his language ability and vocabulary to a level of genius. On the other hand, an eight-year-old who has never spoken or heard any language will struggle to acquire even the most basic vocabulary. This is yet more proof that stimulation of the basic skills during the first three years is important to ensure further development in the older child.

FIGURE 1: The Neuron

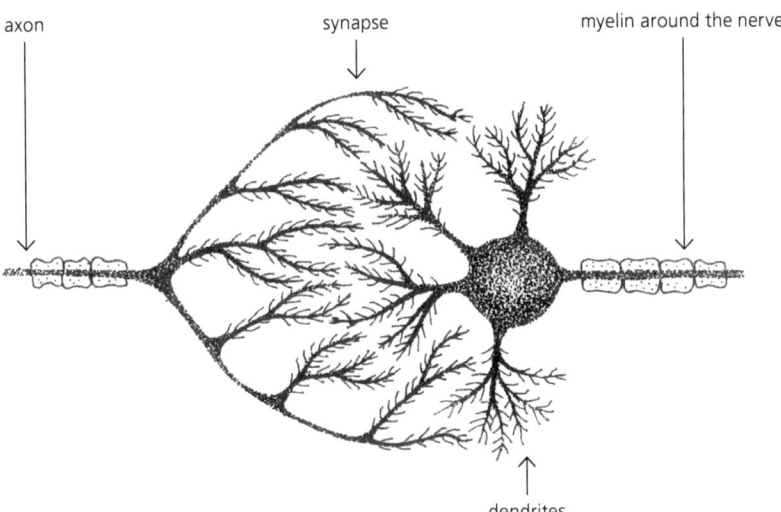

Many people use IQ tests (determining of the intelligence quotient) to measure potential. Apart from the fact that IQ test results can be altered by doing the correct 'exercises', some other arguments also dismiss the use of these tests for measuring potential. IQ tests do not measure the natural dimensions of the human intellect, but are merely an indicator of a certain stage of intellectual development in specific areas. These tests can be used to measure development in those areas, and form the basis for improving and developing those abilities, but cannot be employed to measure the full intellectual ability of either a child or an adult. Certain aspects of human functioning, such as the ability to solve practical problems and to take responsibility, are not taken into account by these tests, even though they are important abilities that can influence a person's functioning, either positively or negatively. Other functions, such as social skills and perseverance, can have a direct influence on performance and achievement, but are not measured by the tests. IQ tests are, in other words, a valuable way of measuring abilities with regard to specific aspects of development, but cannot be employed to indicate human potential.

There are many reasons why we do not utilise and develop our full potential, but most importantly it is a lack of knowledge about:
- the brain and its potential
- the ways that the brain functions can be employed to learn and memorise more efficiently

- the integration of the various brain functions
- the emotional needs of children and adults
- the role that both parents play in the development of the child
- the different education styles and parental types

Apart from unutilised potential, the general functioning and adaptation of children and adults are further limited by insufficient communication and support within the family.

The learning process

A newborn baby has plenty to learn from his new environment and from the world around him. The processes by which a baby, child or adult learns, are based on certain principles that stay the same throughout his life. There are, however, various external influences that can simplify, speed up, slow down or block the process.

Although the basic learning process takes place in the brain, it cannot happen without stimuli from the rest of the body. The stimuli coming from the various body organs, and from the environment outside the body, are transported to specific areas in the brain by means of electrical impulses travelling along the nervous system. These impulses cause a chemical reaction in the specific brain area. The chemical reaction sends a message to a body part or organ, where a reaction occurs. The environmental stimuli are called the *input* to the brain. The processing of this input information is known as *integration*, while the reaction on the stimuli is called the *output*. For example, when you read here, the words on the page are the visual input. The symbols and letters that your brain processes into words are the integration, and your reaction (whether you read faster or more slowly, or put the book down; whether you like what you read or feel negative about it) is the output.

Different parts of the brain are responsible for processing different stimuli. In other words, a specific brain area is equipped for specific functions. The following are the most basic brain areas (see figure 2):

1. After the spinal cord, the **brain stem** is the most primitive part of the brain. It is responsible for the total mass patterns of movement, in other words, the big or gross body and limb movements (e.g. rolling over).
2. The **cerebral hemispheres, or midbrain** is responsible for individualistic motor patterns (e.g. throwing a ball at a target) and the fine motor movements (e.g. writing).
3. The **cerebral cortex** is responsible for the higher cognitive functions, such as memory and reasoning. The shape and construction of this brain part distinguish us from animals. This is the main part employed for studying.
4. **Sensory-motor integration** is the process responsible for movement patterns, enabling us to efficiently react to environmental stimuli. The sensory impulses from the

sense organs, and the motor impulses from the muscles and joints integrate (work together) to bring about the proper reaction. For example, you *see* (sensory impulse) a moving ball and you *catch* (motor action of the muscles) the ball. You will not be able to catch the ball unless the message that you receive from the eyes and the message that is sent to the muscles are integrated.

5. **The limbic system** is a combination of brain areas that supports the processing of emotions. Emotions such as sorrow, shame, joy and pride are registered in the limbic area, and your responses to these are controlled by the limbic system.
6. **The reticular formation** receives impulses from sense and body organs, and plays a role in the state of alertness. Various impulses coming from the environment and from the different organs influence this formation and determine whether you are awake, drowsy or asleep. Your state of alertness plays an important role in your ability to concentrate and to study.

FIGURE 2: The basic brain areas

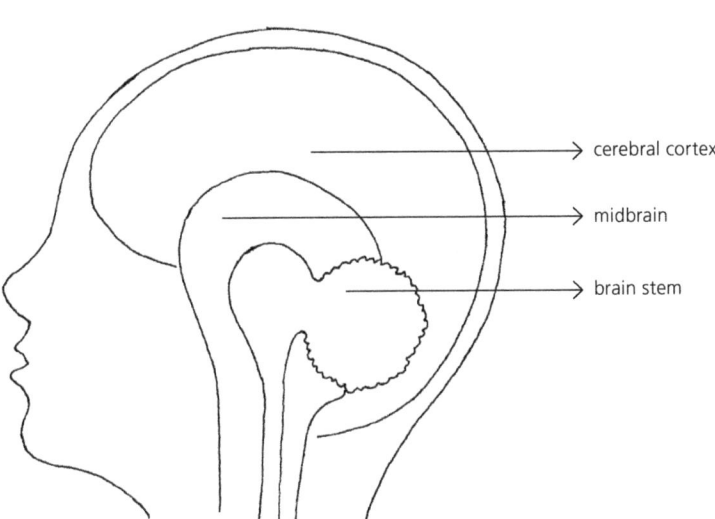

Not only does *each part* of the brain need stimulation, but the different parts also need to be *integrated* in order to effectuate appropriate responses. A well-adapted person will respond in the appropriate manners.

Stimulation

The beginning of the learning process is the first step towards developing potential. When the brain learns, it gets stimulated, encouraging the formation of connections. This includes all forms of learning, such as memorising, recalling information, understanding information, emotional control and social interactions. In a well-adjusted person these functions are well integrated, resulting in appropriate responses.

Here is an example:

A few days after a baby boy is born, he experiences hunger pangs and does not know what to make of them. He becomes anxious, cries and then gets picked up (sense of touch) and fed (hunger pangs disappear and are replaced with a pleasant sensation). The baby has now learned that when he cries, somebody will respond and pick him up and take care of him. He feels safe and experiences pleasant sensations in the form of touch (he gets picked up) and auditory perceptions (his mother's comforting voice). The unpleasant sensation of hunger disappears (he is fed) and a positive, emotional reaction takes its place (I am significant, I am taken care of, I am safe). The next time he experiences hunger pangs, he will cry again to get rid of them.

Another example:

A 10-month-old baby girl sees (visual sensation) a small chair. As she has previously had the experience and exercise of crawling towards the chair (gross motor movement) and standing up against the chair (balance), she does it again. Balance, which is constantly improved by exercise, enables her to lift one leg and carry her weight on one foot. Strong hip muscles, and practised trunk rotation movements, enable her to put one knee on the chair. Well-developed hand and shoulder muscles, together with the hip muscles, enable her to pull herself up and climb onto the chair. Practised rotation movements enable her to turn around and sit down. A learning process based on previous experiences and exercise, as well as the integration of sensations, has taken place. This is the result of a stimulating environment. When the various sensory systems are stimulated by exposing them to different experiences, integration takes place, paving the way for further development of movement patterns and learning.

Stimulation of the sensory systems plays an important part in the child's development and adaptation. Here are some examples of the effects that stimulation has on a child:

- Stimulated children enjoy acquiring new skills and are eager to learn.
- Stimulated children have been exposed to a variety of experiences and are keen to discover new ones. They are confident and daring.
- Stimulated children have a vast 'library' of information that can be used for comparing new information and experiences. They are well-adapted and creative.
- Stimulated children evoke positive responses and comments from other people, feel positive about others, act with confidence and communicate efficiently. They have good social skills.
- Thanks to previous experiences, stimulated children understand many of the events and concepts in their environment. They are regarded as intelligent.
- Thanks to emotional coaching, stimulated children understand other people and their emotions. They are emotionally mature.
- Stimulated children have the elements to develop a healthy self-image and feel good about themselves. They have a more positive lookout on life and on problems.
- A healthy self-image and positive attitude allow stimulated children to tackle problems confidently and enthusiastically, resulting in more efficient problem-solving.
- Stimulated children have many advantages over children who are mostly left to themselves.
- Stimulated children have a much better chance to become well-adapted, successful adults than unstimulated children.
- Stimulated children are generally happy children.

These aspects should convince any parent to stimulate his or her child, and to expose him to a stimulating environment. A stimulated child learns to optimally utilise his brain. The human brain is particularly adaptable and can store and process huge amounts of information. However, in order to optimally utilise the brain, it needs to be optimally stimulated.

Brain development begins in the womb, and it is interesting to see what takes place prenatally. The moment the mother finds out that she is pregnant, she can begin to optimally stimulate her baby. Note that that does not mean she now has to keep her child busy with expensive educational toys day and night. If the parent knows and understands what stimulation really means, it can be done all day long during everyday household chores – and emotional coaching can take place continually. Efficient stimulation will help your child develop into a well-adapted, balanced and happy human being who will make a positive contribution to his society.

---

1. T. Buzan, *Use both sides of your brain*. (USA: Plume 1991).

3

The stimulating environment

Genes versus environment

During the 1940s, the American psychiatrist René Spitz investigated the role of the environment in the development of a child. This marked the beginning of the continued debate on the role of heredity versus the environment. Spitz studied underprivileged babies in two groups. The first group grew up in a so-called home for castaway babies, while the second group consisted of babies whose mothers were in jail and who were taken care of in an orphanage on the prison grounds.

Although the two institutions appeared the same outwardly (both were clean, with acceptable food, clothes and medical care), there was a huge difference in the amount of care and stimulation that each of them offered. Babies in the prison orphanage were fed and taken care of by their own mothers, receiving plenty of love and attention. These children's development was normal, even though they grew up in an orphanage. In contrast to this, children in the home for castaway babies received very little stimulation because there was only one nurse for every eight babies. Apart from the brief feedings and nappy changes, each baby was isolated in his own cot, the sides of which were covered with sheets to prevent the spreading of germs and diseases! With nothing to look at or to play with, and – worst of all – minimal contact and love from other human beings, these babies suffered grossly, many of them dying before the age of two. Those who did survive were physically underdeveloped, highly prone to infections and seriously mentally retarded. At the age of three, most of them could still not walk or talk, and in contrast to the happy children of the prison orphanage, they were noticeably reserved and apathetic.

With this research, Spitz proved that early care and stimulation are crucially important for a child's development. Psychologists who support these behaviour theories and have done their own research, have come to the same conclusion.

Today we tend to lean towards the opposite side, as molecular biologists shed more light on our chromosomes every day in an effort to prove that these are responsible for diseases such as alcoholism, Alzheimer's, various types of cancer, and so forth. Although genes are important, Lise Eliot, in her book *What's Going On In There?*, points out that nerve cells, and therefore also the brain, are particularly adaptable.[1] The brain is a living, dynamic organ that constantly adapts to the demands of the environment and never stops developing.

Children who had been exposed to sound stimulation programmes between the ages of four months and five years, obtained a better outcome in mathematical and reading skill tests at the age of 15 and generally had a higher IQ than children who had not received efficient stimulation.[2] Stimulation programmes that were introduced after the age of five had no positive influence on either the child's IQ or his academic performance. Eliot says, "The brain is without doubt our most fascinating organ. Parents, educators, and society as a whole have tremendous power to shape the wrinkly universe inside each child's head, and, with it, the kind of person he or she will turn out to be. We owe it to our children to help them grow the best brains possible."[3]

Intelligence cannot be predicted, nor can it be predetermined, but it is influenced by the environment and environmental events that take place during the first three years of a child's life. That is why stimulation is so utterly important during this critical period of development. Efficient early stimulation can alter the size, structure and chemical functioning of a baby's brain.[4] While nature provides the child with the potential to grow and succeed, it is the environment that allows him to grow and to reach maturity. Although the environment cannot remove genetic traits, it does have the ability to promote and to develop a child's potential.

One important aspect that influences early development, is the time and attention that parents devote to their child. Time is precious and should be utilised efficiently. If you are going to spend time with your child, make sure that you get the most out of it and that it indeed benefits his development. Here are some of the effects that environment has on a child:

- Good interpersonal relations with other people, and particularly relatives, encourage a child to enjoy contact with others and to develop from an egocentric baby into a child who heeds other people's feelings.

- While emotional fulfilment encourages healthy interpersonal relations, emotional rejection by family members often leads to personality disorders.
- The method of child education plays an important role – the democratic style promoting personal and social adaptation.
- Because the brain uses the same systems for processing music as it does for perceptions, memory and language, exposure to music has an influence on the other abilities. In fact, music is particularly beneficial for brain development, having a positive effect on motor, mathematical and reading skills.
- The importance of talking to your baby cannot be overemphasised. The more words a child hears, the sooner he learns to talk.
- The environment also plays a part in emotional control. The child is best influenced when a carer follows the emotional coaching method.[5] So if your child has a carer other than the mother, not only his physical care, but also the total emotional milieu that is created within the caring environment, should be taken into account.

Hopefully you will decide to take the responsibility for your child's stimulation – and a sound stimulation programme – upon yourself. However, if this is not feasible, you should make sure that the carer you choose is knowledgeable and competent enough to take care of your child's stimulation in your absence. Your own high standards regarding your child's stimulation and education should not be compromised.

How does stimulation take place?

Stimulating your child means that you will provide tasks, games, objects and/or equipment (toys) that can be used or manipulated in such a way that he will learn something in order to develop a new skill that has not been used before. This way the child's brain is stimulated and new dendrites or connections are formed. To maintain these new dendrites and make them a permanent part of the brain, the newly acquired skill needs to be practised and repeated.

The child can be stimulated by teaching him a new task. The parent or carer chooses a task and teaches it to the child step by step. The child is then given the opportunity to practise the task, honing his new skill. The child learns, for example, to sing a new song, to use a spoon for self-feeding or to catch a ball.

Another method of stimulation is to provide equipment and/or toys which will invite the child, in an informal manner, to play and to learn new skills in the process. The child repeats the newly acquired skill, improving his ability. The child may, for instance, discover a ball in the playroom and by his own initiative begin to kick, pick up and throw the ball. Without guidance he might well improve his skill, but with specific guidance, and through your example, it will happen faster and more efficiently.

The child can also be stimulated by watching other people perform a specific task. A new skill is then acquired by imitation. A good example is the acquisition of language. The child listens to the parents' conversations and imitates the sounds and words, gradually building a vocabulary and language skill. A child quickly learns by imitation, which can sometimes be embarrassing when he picks up the parents' bad habits and repeats them in the company of strangers!

With little time at their disposal, parents often want to stimulate their child as efficiently as possible, in the shortest possible time. That is why it is important to create a stimulating environment in which the child can spontaneously discover new skills, but where newly acquired skills can also be practised regularly – with or without direct parental input. A stimulating environment also affords a child the opportunity to make his own discoveries and to use the available toys and equipment in creative ways. In this way he also learns to keep himself busy.

A stimulating environment

A stimulating environment is an environment, and circumstances, that stimulate or incite certain processes in a person. A child's environment should invite him to take part in different tasks. It should arouse his curiosity and enthusiasm to such an extent that he feels eager to take on a task, using his existing skills and acquiring new ones.

The environment should give the child the opportunity to learn. Not only must he be able to acquire new skills, but also to use and 'practise' existing skills in order to improve them. If an environment consists of objects which the child already knows well, where he has already acquired all possible skills and where he knows all the possibilities of each object, it has become a place where he will feel safe, but where he will not be stimulated to take on new challenges.

A stimulating environment, on the other hand, is an environment where the child sees the possibility of participating in a task which is unknown to him, yet seems to be within his capabilities. This incites the child to think how he will go about the task, encouraging him to participate so that learning can take place. The child's environment should contain aspects which make him feel safe (i.e. mostly familiar, with tasks that he can perform with confidence), but at the same time be stimulating in order to encourage the discovery of new abilities (i.e. partly unfamiliar, interesting and challenging).

A stimulating environment …
- is inviting
- arouses curiosity
- creates expectations
- offers the opportunity to learn, utilise abilities, practise new skills, use different senses and integrate abilities

In a young child, the environment should incite as many senses as possible, preventing the synapses and dendrites from falling into disuse and getting 'pruned'.

Here are some examples of how each sense can be incited by the environment:

- **Vision:** Colours, shapes, sizes, dimensions, numbers, movement
- **Hearing:** Rhythm, sounds, music, words, language, voices, noise, sounds from nature, animal sounds, rhymes
- **Touch:** Textures, body parts, food/objects in the mouth, temperature, movement on the skin, light touch, deep pressure, incidental/direct contact
- **Taste:** Food, objects
- **Smell:** People, objects, food, herbs, plants and nature, pets, environment
- **Motor:** Nervous impulses from muscles, joints, skin, ears, movement, deep pressure
    » Gross motorial, i.e. where almost the whole body is involved, for example:
        - Movement: levels of movement as on a swing and in a pram (rotation, forward, backward, sideward, vertical, horizontal)
        - Balance: static, dynamic, moving basis
        - Carrying weight: on hips, shoulders, legs, arms, hands, feet
    » Fine motorial, i.e. where mainly the hands and fingers are involved, as in clay play, picking up or stringing beads, using a pencil, using cutlery
- **Emotions:** All the above areas of stimulation have an emotional component. No one sense is used in isolation – they are always integrated with other senses and with an emotional reaction.

Integrating all these aspects into your child's stimulating environment seems almost impossible, but when the different aspects of development are discussed later on in the book, you will learn practical ways of including these aspects in the daily stimulation and upbringing of your baby and/or child. An understanding of the basic principle of stimulation, combined with a sound knowledge of your child's abilities, will make stimulating your child come naturally and easily.

Your relationship with your child

The most important aspect of stimulation is the intimate relationship between the parent/carer and the child. The quality of the time that you spend together will improve when the following principles are applied:

1. Choose an activity that both you and your child will enjoy – a child quickly senses when a parent is bored, when his or her mind is not in the game, or when he or she does not enjoy the time with the child. If you choose something that the child does

not want to do, he will not pay attention, make unnecessary mistakes, try to divert your attention, refuse to cooperate or generally get your dander up.

2. Make regular eye contact – it brings about a feeling of significance in the child. Think of your own frustration when you try to convey important information and the other person refuses to look up from the book that he or she is reading. When the person does put down the book and pay attention to what you say (i.e. make eye contact), you feel as if you matter. The same goes for your child. When you play with your child but are more interested in the conversation that you are having with your friend at the same time, all three parties soon become annoyed.

3. Touch your child – we all know the effect that a timely hug has on ourselves. We should remember that with our children too. It is sometimes better to take him firmly by the arm or around the waist, turn his head towards you and say his name before you start talking. Merely raising your voice and looking disheartened because he will not listen to you, makes the child feel insecure and can be extremely frustrating for the parent.

4. Forget about your other obligations – 10 minutes of undivided attention can sometimes win you an hour to get your own things done. Divided attention often leads to feelings of inadequacy in both parties, as well as frustrations because no task gets done properly.

5. Compliment your child and criticise him in a constructive way so that your comment teaches him something positive, rather than making him feel like a failure. This young age is the best time to ensure that your child develops a healthy self-image and self-esteem.

6. Lay down clear guidelines and boundaries – your child must understand that some behaviours are impermissible. Make sure that he knows exactly what is desirable, what is acceptable and what is not. Unacceptable behaviour can be punished by using moderate control. Also teach your child what other people may find unacceptable – your child may, for instance, climb on the old chair in your living room, but not on other people's furniture.

7. Apply discipline consistently. Knowing where he stands gives a child direction and makes him feel confident and secure.

8. Most importantly, your child must have a good time. Children, and possibly also adults, learn and develop faster if enjoyment forms part of the learning process. Your child's happy face, while enjoying a task, is of the utmost importance if you are to get the most out of the time you spend together. If not, switch to another task or change the circumstances. Re-evaluate the situation, making sure that the child enjoys it.

The choice of play

When choosing a game to play with your child, ask yourself the following questions in order to establish what you would really like to achieve:

1. Which *aspect* of development would you like to stimulate? You may be teaching your child a motor skill such as rolling a ball, or an auditory skill like listening to a nursery rhyme. Knowing what the object of the game is will enable you to assess the child's participation and progress more efficiently, so that the necessary adjustments can be made.
2. What is *the child's ability* with regard to this aspect of development? If you know that a child has difficulty with a task, offer it at a level that he will find easy and enjoyable. Knowing your child's ability will ensure that you can make positive comments afterwards, leaving the child with a feeling of:
   'I can' and
   'I have made my parent happy'.
   This feeling builds a positive self-image. A feeling of failure in the child and an expression of annoyance, or even shame, on the parent's face when the child cannot master a task, is destructive for his self-image.
3. What are *the child's previous experiences* of the circumstances? If he has never played with a ball, he will experience more difficulties than if he regularly plays with balls of different sizes. The same applies if he has never played on lawn or in a place where other people watch him and make comments. His ability and response will differ according to his familiarity with the circumstances. Be supportive in unfamiliar circumstances, excuse errors and do not push the child if he needs time to orientate himself.
4. What are *the circumstances* in the direct environment? In other words, what is the input that the child receives from the environment? You may be surprised to see what the child is exposed to – there could be loud noise, strangers, bright light, or the child could be hungry, thirsty or tired. The child's response and participation can also be affected by input from other parts of the body, like an empty stomach.
5. How does *the child respond*, in other words what is the output? That will give you an indication of how the child experiences the task, whether he enjoys it or whether it scares or bores him. A learning process in the form of input, output and integration should be taking place. If not, try to identify the cause of the problem. It is no good persisting with a task if the child has lost interest – he will not be learning anything and you will both experience frustration instead of stimulation and enjoyment.
6. Which aspect is the child learning or practising that will *promote development*? Encourage the child to make adjustments while performing the task. He should either show improvement in a certain aspect of the task, learn something extra or practise existing skills in order to improve them. If the child merely repeats tasks without

making adjustments, he learns nothing and becomes bored. Take painting as example: He can do something new each time – mix colours, touch the paint, use his fingers, use different brushes, add more or less water, paint over different textures, paint on his body, learn the name of a colour, or use the brush and paint pot more efficiently. These adjustments need not necessarily be initiated by the adult – children often make the discoveries themselves. The adult's task is to make sure that a learning process is indeed taking place.

7. Which *functions are being integrated*, resulting in stimulation? Painting can again be taken as example: The child can merely learn to handle the brush, or many other functions can be stimulated at the same time. Consider these functions which are stimulated when your child paints:
   - Touch stimulation: feels brush in hand, touches paint, touches paper or fabric being painted, feels paint on skin when painting his body
   - Posture control: maintains standing or sitting position
   - Auditory: follows instructions and basic rules
   - Balance: maintains body position
   - Coordination: manipulates paintbrush using either gross shoulder movements or fine finger movements (depending on age), plays with fingers in paint, paints along outlines of figures
   - Body image: learns to use arms efficiently, learns body parts when painting on his body or painting a human figure (older child)
   - Lateralisation: still uses both hands or begins to develop a dominant hand
   - Integration between the two body sides: uses both hands at once for finger painting; older child begins to lateralise spontaneously, developing a dominant hand
   - Crossing the body midline: after lateralisation child either paints on one side of midline only or dominant hand crosses to other side of body
   - Visual perception: observes shapes shown to him, observes parent painting different shapes and figures, begins to paint own shapes, e.g. 'ball' = circle
   - Recognising, grouping and identifying of colours and shapes
   - Creative ability: completes task on own initiative: (Being task orientated, the end result is of little significance to the young child. Other people's opinions about what he has tried to do, e.g. experimenting with colours until everything looks like a black mess, often suppress his creative ability, leading to an early conviction that he cannot draw and a consequent withdrawal from this activity.)

As a parent, you may be surprised at how many different functions can be stimulated by a simple task like painting. Analysing each game or activity in this way should convince you that there is no reason to buy expensive educational toys. In order to stimulate your child efficiently, however, you will need to broaden you knowledge and apply your common sense!

Every chapter in this book contains games and activities which are aimed at stimulating specific aspects of development. However, more often than not, various different abilities are stimulated while performing a single task.

Proper stimulation makes for happy children who are eager to learn and take on new challenges. Your child will enjoy performing tasks with you, feeling involved and secure while constantly being exposed to new challenges and learning opportunities. The different tasks stimulate development, ensuring successful learning. And what is more, you as a parent will find joy in spending time with your child!

Toys

To make sure that your child's environment contains the necessary equipment to stimulate him or her at different ages, I have made a list of toys that are important for each development stage up to about three years of age. You may want to extend the list, or make many of the toys yourself if you find that you cannot afford to buy everything.

- Papier-mâché is cheap to make (see recipes in appendix 2, page 157) and can be used for making shapes, shape-sorters, simple jigsaw puzzles, fantasy toys like human figures and animals, musical instruments such as rattles, simple furniture and household items like spoons, cups and plates. Decorated with poster paint and an added layer of varnish, the toys will be surprisingly durable and hard-wearing.
- Books can be made out of cardboard (using sturdy cereal boxes for the covers), waste fabric and/or paper, together with pictures from old magazines.
- Make different sized balls by stuffing old socks or pantihose with firmly crumpled newsprint. Make sure that the balls are nice and round so that they will roll easily.
- Cans, plastic containers and empty plastic bottles can be used for scooping and pouring sand and water. Pierce holes in the bottoms of some containers so that they can serve as sieves. Keeping the lids of plastic containers will allow the child to sort and match the lids to their corresponding containers, while different sizes will teach him the concepts of bigger, smaller, heavier and lighter. These containers can also be used as bath toys.
- Waste fabric can be used for making rag dolls and soft toys. (Waste fabric is ideal, as it often yields different and interesting textures.) Use the filling from old pillows and duvets as stuffing.

Although shiny and expensive toys may impress friends and relatives, they are certainly not indispensable for efficient stimulation of your child.

Newborn babies

- Snugly wrap your baby in a *soft flannelette* or *muslin blanket* to make him feel secure.
- The baby must hear his *parent's voices*. Continue using the *music* that you sang and played before your baby's birth.
- Use *pictures of shapes* in clearly distinguishable shades such as black, white and grey, as well as bright colours in combination with white, inside your baby's cot, placing them approximately 20 cm from his face. Looking at them while lying awake will stimulate the brain parts for the registration and interpretation of vision, which develop rapidly during the first few months of his life. The *mother's* and *father's faces* are also important – holding your baby close to your body as often as possible will allow him to study your face. It is a precious experience to watch your tiny baby earnestly examining your face and to realise that this is one of the very first visual images to be captured in his little brain!
- Guard against overstimulating your baby in the first few weeks of his life by regularly *minimising stimuli* (such as noises, strangers or unfamiliar visual images) during waking and sleeping times. A baby needs time to process new information. Remove him from unfamiliar environments when he becomes restless – an overly stimulated baby is whiny and agitated.
- *Baby massage* is a good idea. Studying this and learning the right techniques will be well worth your while.

Babies who cannot sit up yet

- Provide *different textures* – such as fluffy, smooth, shiny, silky, coarse, hard, soft, wet and dry – for the baby to play on. Lay him down and wrap him in different fabrics. Use different textures in the bath for washing and drying your baby. (Just keep in mind that his skin is still very delicate, and new textures should be introduced gradually and with great care.)
- Introduce the baby to *different movements* by laying him down on a blanket or towel. Holding the four corners, the parents then rock him in different directions. Or, holding him in your arms, you can rock him, turn him around or move him up and down. Begin by holding him snugly against your body and moving slowly. As he becomes more accustomed to the movement and begins to enjoy the game, you can hold him further away, making the movements faster and bigger. Warning: This game could excite your baby, so do not play it before bedtime!
- Hang *different shapes* and *objects* above the baby's cot or cradle where he can look at them. They can be anything that you buy in a toy shop, although cheaper household items that can be alternated daily may be a better option. As your baby gets older and begins to wave his arms, you can lower the objects so that he touches them, learning that his movement causes a reaction. This will encourage more movement

and investigation of objects, which in turn leads to reaching out and seizing objects. You can, for instance, alternate different spoons, plastic cups in different sizes and colours, shiny foil dishes that will cause an interesting noise when touched, and paper balls. A normal household yields endless possibilities – just use your imagination. These objects could actually provide more stimulation than beautiful, expensive, soft toys that differ very little in appearance. *Music* (as will be discussed in more detail later) can be used to provide stimulation in more than one way – your baby can listen to it, or you can hold him while rhythmically moving, rocking or dancing with the music, fostering an awareness of its rhythm.

- *Language* is important. Parents should often talk to, and near, their baby.
- As soon as a baby can hold *small objects* in his hands, he will further investigate them by putting them in his mouth, which has many nerve endings that enable him to observe the objects very closely. Provide clean objects that will not hurt your baby, rather than trying to keep them out of his mouth. These may be toys or household items like teaspoons, plastic containers, plastic cups or mugs, scarves, small bottles and clothes with different textures. They should be washed regularly before being given to the baby to investigate.
- *Fabric* or *plastic books* are handy for this development stage, as the baby can hold and investigate them by himself without tearing them or choking on paper that has become pulp in his mouth. Introduce your baby to paper books by turning the pages for him and talking about the pictures – he will soon start making noises in an attempt to 'join in the conversation'.
- Hold your baby in your arms often, as you would during feedings, and regulary lay him down on his back and stomach (i.e. in *different positions*) at waking times. Lay your baby down on *different textures* and put toys around him, encouraging him to reach out, roll over and start moving. The toys should differ in colour, shape, size and texture and some should make a noise when moved, rolled or pressed. Again, there is no need for expensive toys – use everyday household items, as long as they will not hurt the baby while he investigates.
- Baby massage can now be extended to include slow *stretch movements*.
- Encourage *kicking movements* by holding an object near the baby's feet that will make a noise when he kicks against it. Babies like kicking in the bath, and when a baby is held to stand on his feet on your lap, the normal reflex will cause treading movements that will strengthen the legs and condition the feet to carry his weight.

Babies who can sit on their own

Continue using all the equipment and methods mentioned for the previous two stages. At this stage, the baby will have learned to roll over and change his position without help. However, the movements in different planes and in different positions should still continue in order to stimulate balance, without which the child will not be able to crawl and walk.

- The baby should now be laid down *on his stomach* more frequently, with or without a rolled-up towel as support under his shoulders. This position forces him to lift up his head, strengthening the back neck muscles and preparing him for crawling.
- The baby now enjoys different faces and recognises many different people. A *mirror* could keep him busy for a while when lying on his stomach. *Photographs* of faces will also interest him.
- The baby enjoys *moving toys,* such as windmills, jack-in-the-box and balls, as well as toys that cause a reaction when being hit or kicked. *Soap bubbles* could keep him entertained for some time, while reaching out to touch them also encourages the use of both hands. *Blocks* bring endless pleasure when the parent builds a tower and the baby is allowed to knock it over. Hitting two blocks together, or clapping hands, also teaches the two sides of the body to work together in a coordinated way.
- Toys that are put *just outside the baby's reach* when lying on his stomach, encourage him to stretch out his arms, move forward and eventually start to crawl.
- The baby enjoys language and is particularly stimulated by *rhymes* and *rhythmic movements*. Although he cannot actively take part in these yet, it is important to make them part of your daily routine. Be sure to include rhymes and games that will teach him the names of the body parts.
- The baby now begins to use his hands and fingers more efficiently and soon learns to let go of objects that he is holding. He enjoys sticking his fingers into holes in toys and should be watched so as not to get hurt in case they get stuck. Provide toys with bigger openings, like *shape-sorters*, that can be investigated with the fingers.
- In the sitting position the baby is now ready to develop his fine motor coordination, i.e. the use of his hands and fingers. He uses his fingers to initially pick up *larger* and later also *smaller objects* and manipulate them in his hands.
- The baby enjoys shaking *rattles* and *other musical instruments*. Encourage him to use both hands, stimulating the collaboration between the two sides of the body. Fill *bottles* and *containers with small beads and seeds*, taking care that the lids are secure, as the baby can choke if he puts the small objects into his mouth.
- Exercise the baby's eye movements by moving *small objects* in different directions (i.e. up, down, left, right, diagonally and in a circle) in front of him.
- The baby now enjoys playing *hiding games*. The parent can hide and appear from behind a screen, or hide toys under a blanket, allowing the baby to remove the blanket and 'discover' the toys. Or cover your baby with a light blanket, encouraging him to pull it off himself.
- The baby also enjoys *unpacking*. Access to a kitchen cupboard with unbreakables will encourage him to unpack and throw articles about, happily exploring and making plenty of noise.
- The baby enjoys *sand* and *water play* and although this can be a messy affair, exposure to these elements is vital for the development of a baby's sense of touch.

You can also make *finger paint* or *play goo* (see recipes in appendix 2, page 158), dress your baby in old clothes and allow him to play to his heart's content. Weather permitting, he can play in his nappy only, exposing his whole body to the different textures of the paint and goo.

Crawling babies

Continue using all the games and equipment mentioned for the previous stages. Using your initiative, alternate the toys (including household items) regularly, exposing your baby to a variety of stimuli. Crawling is an important stage of development which should be encouraged – do not wish for your baby to start walking too soon!

- *Games that encourage crawling*, such as 'chasing' each other, crawling after a ball or simply crawling from one room in the house to the other, exercise this action, stimulating the balance and coordination that a baby needs for walking. As the baby normally enjoys his new-found mobility and freedom to go wherever he likes, little encouragement is needed to get him moving.
- With the baby's body image now further developing, he must learn to compare his own size to that of *objects in the environment*. That happens while crawling underneath objects of different sizes (chairs and tables), crawling and clambering over objects (a stack of cushions on the floor) and passing between objects. Although toys such as tunnels and tents will encourage this, the average home offers numerous challenges for the crawling baby. Guard against too many restrictions as to what he may and may not do. These activities also promote the development of concepts such as *into*, *out of*, *inside*, *outside*, *on top*, *underneath* and *next to*.
- With the fine motor skills continuing to develop, you can now give your baby smaller objects to manipulate. Give him *blocks* to throw into a container, *plastic bowls* to stack and fit together, *one-piece wooden jigsaw puzzles* to try, and lids to cover and uncover *containers*, promoting concepts such as *into*, *out of*, *inside*, *outside*, *on top*, *underneath* and *next to*. The baby will now constantly be unpacking cupboards, exploring everything that is inside, often resulting in the contents being strewn all over the house. Once again, giving him access to one cupboard or box with safe, permitted articles will save you the trouble of having to tidy your entire house night after night. Regularly alternate the objects in the cupboard or box to prevent boredom.
- The baby will soon start *pulling himself up against furniture*, carrying weight on his legs. This is good exercise that should not be discouraged. Make sure that your house provides enough opportunities for your baby to safely move along furniture without injuring himself when he falls (by removing a coffee table with sharp corners that could hurt his head, for instance).
- The baby can now *hold and let go* with ease, and he understands the concept of *action and reaction*. This could result in an endless game that parents may find quite boring: seizing and throwing a toy, then crying or screaming for the parent to pick

it up, only to throw it down again. This teaches your baby to hold and let go and develops his perspective (the toy becomes smaller as it moves further away). He also learns that he is able to manipulate the environment somehow.
- The time is now right for the baby to *push around* somewhat heavier objects (like a box of toys), exercising his legs and hips, as well as his arms and shoulders. This is good exercise for the walking action. Keep in mind that wheel carts may move too fast, causing the baby to fall.
- With your baby's knowledge of his body now extending, he can point out a number of body parts, initially by imitating the parent, but later also independently when asked.

Walking toddlers

A child rather than a baby, the toddler actively explores the world, fiddling with everything that he sees. Continue using the games and equipment for the previous stages. The chapters covering the various aspects of development contain more examples of suitable games.
- The toddler's motor development remains an important aspect, as it also leads to the development of other concepts. Give your child ample opportunity to *crawl, roll, swing, run, jump, climb* and *clamber*, including exposure to different textures as well as to language, music and rhythm. Although there are excellent toys and equipment available on the market, the furniture in your house will do just fine – you may, in fact, find that your toddler uses the furniture anyway, no matter how expensive the equipment that you have bought for his playroom!
- With the fine coordination further developing, your toddler can now manipulate one-piece jigsaw puzzles, for instance, with greater ease. He also learns to hold and manipulate *writing instruments* such as *pencils* and *paintbrushes*, begins to feed himself and learns to use a spoon.
- The toddler now *integrates the various skills* that he has acquired, allowing more efficient participation in activities, like fitting shapes into a shape-sorter, remembering where things are kept and concentrating on a task for longer periods.
- The toddler becomes *more independent* and insists on doing things, like eating and undressing by himself. He also favours choosing his own toys and food. These activities are no less important than any of the others used for the stimulation of specific aspects of development.

THE PLAYROOM

The toddler should have the following basic toys available in his playroom:

Inside:
- Balls of different sizes
- Cars or similar toys that can be manipulated
- Blunt-nosed scissors for the older toddler
- A cupboard or container for storing toys
- Plastic containers with lids (various sizes)
- Wooden blocks in different sizes
- Shape-sorters and one-piece jigsaw puzzles for fitting shapes into the correct openings
- Books for reading to the child
- Hard-wearing books for 'reading' by himself
- Music for teaching him songs and rhythm
- Background music, such as baroque
- Musical instruments to be used as desired
- A quiet corner to retreat to when he feels sad or overstimulated or just wants to be alone
- A place (or item) to get rid of emotions like anger, e.g. a pillow or punch bag that can be hit when feeling frustrated
- Household items (or toys resembling household items), such as cups, plates, food, a broom and others, that can be used for imitating the parent in the house
- Dolls with clothes and blankets
- A toy workbench with a hammer
- A mirror at a height where he can see his own image
- A place for painting and scribbling, for example, a blackboard, a piece of paper stuck to the wall or a small table with papers where she can experiment
- Old magazines to tear and cut, and for showing and finding pictures

Outside:
- A lawn with sun and shade spots
- A sandpit with water and containers in different sizes
- A place for climbing and clambering, perhaps a jungle gym
- Swings
- Plants and a vegetable patch for watering plants, picking flowers or vegetables and watching insects and birds
- A pet of some kind, to teach him to consider and care for others

1. L. Eliot, *What's Going On In There?* (New York: Bantam Books, 1999).
2. L.J. Schweinhart and D.P. Weilkart, 'The Effects of the Perry Preschool Program on Youths through Age 15 – a Summary', in: Consortium for Longitudinal Studies Staff, *As the Twig Is Bent: Lasting Effects of Preschool Programs* (Hillsdale, New Jersey: Lawrence Erlbaum Associates, 1983), 7–101.
3. L. Eliot, *What's Going On In There?*
4. Ibid.
5. J. Gottman, *The Heart of Parenting* (London: Bloomsbury Publishing, 1997).

4

Brain development

Never ceasing to fascinate me, the prenatal development of the embryo and foetus has to be one of the greatest miracles in the world. In this chapter, I have the pleasure of sharing with you the knowledge that I have acquired during my research. Foetal development will be discussed first, followed by guidelines that the mother can follow during pregnancy in order to promote normal development in her unborn baby.

The development of the nervous system

When talking about the nervous system, I mean the somatosensory system, or sense organs, in particular. Our sense organs are the organs that tell our brains what goes on in our bodies and in our environments. The brain then sends impulses back to the body so that the body can react on the 'messages'. These impulses are electrical impulses travelling through the nerve tracts, just as electricity travels through a wire. The better we react to impulses from the environment, the better we adapt to our environment. An adaptable person is a happy person who is more inclined to be successful.

Brain growth

Brain growth is the result of the formation of 'body maps' in the cerebral cortex. The formation of these maps depends on the electrical activity in the incoming sensory fibres. In other words, the 'messages' or 'input' that is transported by the sensory tracts, or nervous system, from the body or environment to the brain. When this map is formed in our cortex, a specific area of the cortex is allocated to each body part. The size of this area depends on the amount of sensory stimulation, meaning the number of messages coming from a particular body part. When there is no activity (stimulation), and hence no messages coming from this body part, there will only be a very small, or even no, corresponding cortex area.

All the sensations that a baby experiences intrauterly are important in the initial formation of this 'map' in order to shape the child's future body perception. If the basic 'body map' is intact at birth, it can continue to grow and develop, adapting to the child's changing abilities and experiences. Through experience and stimulation different 'maps' are formed in our brains continually, remaining there *for the rest of our lives.*

Different nerves transport different types of messages to different parts of the brain and body. The autonomous nervous system controls the vital organs and functions such as breathing – that we do not think about, and that happen 'automatically'. The central nervous system controls the reactions that we do have control over, e.g. moving a limb. This way pain, light touch, deep pressure, smells, tastes, differences in temperature and sounds can be transported, and we can only become aware of the sensation when the impulse reaches the relevant area in the brain. Although some reactions take place unconsciously, our bodies still react, e.g. by pulling the hand away after a pain stimulus. These 'unconscious' reactions or reflexes are controlled by the lower parts of the brain (spinal cord and brain stem).

Each nerve consists of neurones, interconnected by synapses. A neuron is made up of dendrites, an axon, a cell body, and a synapse with a neurotransmitter (see figure 1) which makes it possible for the impulse to travel through the synapse, transmitting it to the next neuron, or to the relevant brain area. Neurons are differentiated in order to transmit different, and specific, impulses. A light sensation of touch will therefore be transmitted by a certain neuron and a sensation of pain by another. Neuron formation begins in the various ventricles of the brain and happens at an electrifying pace of up to 250 000 per minute! Synapses begin to form in the womb, continuing until the child's second birthday, while neurons are expanded by the growth of more dendrites, 83 per cent of which are formed after birth. That means that the child's cortex triples in density during the first year after birth!

This increase in the number of neurons, axons and dendrites can be compared to the wiring of electrical equipment. The reception of environmental stimuli by the neurons is called 'input', while the brain's reaction on these stimuli, i.e. the impulse that the brain sends out through the neurons, is called 'output'. For example, auditory input takes place when the baby hears a sound, while output happens when he turns his head in the direction of the sound.

While the brain is being wired, the input and output connections are also wired according to the various impulses – visual, language, movement or auditory – that are received. It is interesting to know that after the formation of the initial synapses, these different connections are in competition with one another. Ample activity or stimulation of a synapse leads to molecular changes, resulting in stabilisation of the synapse, while disused synapses degenerate and can eventually die off. In other words, stimulated synapses are retained, while disused synapses disappear. The competition between the synapses is won by those that are stimulated most frequently, while the rest collapse. Eliot describes this process as the 'pruning' of synapses.[1] The body retains only the synapses that are used, that is, those deemed essential for adaptation to the environment. Therefore, a stimulating environment that promotes synapse activity and stimulation is vital for synapse retention and stimulation of brain growth. Healthy brain growth makes for a well-developed brain, which naturally plays a part in intelligence and the ability to adapt. The environment has a direct and permanent effect on the brain structure, and the eventual functioning of the baby's brain.

Nerve myelinisation

Myelinisation of the nerves is another process that affects brain functioning. Myelin is a fatty sheath formed around a nerve (much like the isolation around an electric cable), protecting the nerve against impulses transmitted by other nerves which may interfere with the message, and also accelerating the tempo at which the nerve transmits the message to and from the brain. Although nerve myelinisation starts in the spinal cord five months after conception, the brain only myelinises during the ninth month of pregnancy. As the environment (including diet) affects the tempo and quality of myelinisation, it is important that the baby should take in fat through breast, or full-cream milk up to the age of two years.

The various parts of the brain follow the same process, but at different times. For example, the spinal cord and brain stem are fully myelinised by the time the baby is born, while the midbrain and cerebellum only start myelinising after birth. The subcortical sections of the brain myelinise during the first year of the baby's life, while in the cerebral cortex, the process happens slowly and unevenly – some parts are only myelinised and pruned during the late twenties. No wonder human beings take so long to mature!

Active brain areas

Through various interesting methods researchers have been able to establish which parts of the brain show most activity at a specific age. Activity in a brain area is related to development and growth in that area – that is, the brain area that sends and receives the most impulses. In newborn babies, the brain areas responsible for reflexes, or automatic reactions, are the most active areas. When the baby is two to three months old, the brain areas controlling visual perception are very active, while at six to eight months the areas responsible for cognitive function, emotion and general perception are particularly active. At age seven and eight years the brain reaches its most active stage – experts reckon that brain activity during this period could be double that of an adult!

Critical periods for stimulation

There are critical, optimal periods for the stimulation of any specific brain area. As we already know, stimulated synapses are stabilised to become permanent structures inside the brain, while disused synapses are pruned. This is determined by the experiences and stimulation to which the baby or child is exposed. When the period of synapse stabilisation for a specific brain area elapses without stimulation, the chances of that area being 'rewired' and stimulated become considerably less. The *critical period* for stabilisation has ended.

Different brain areas have different critical periods for stimulation. For example, the critical period for the basic sensory abilities, ends much earlier than the critical period for the more complex skills, such as language and emotions. What is important is that *the critical periods for all the different brain areas begin before the age of four years*. The baby's experiences and stimulation determine which connections are stabilised and retained and which are pruned. In other words, what the brain's permanent wiring – regarding its way of thinking, perception and behaviour – will look like.

The development of the embryo and foetus during the first semester of pregnancy

When the baby is born, he is not a clean sheet of paper. He enters the world with the unique mental skills an abilities needed to fulfil the needs of a newborn baby. A baby's brain is not a miniature version of the adult brain. The nervous system develops in a specific order, from 'head to tail'. At birth, the spinal cord and brain stem (the lower brain structures controlling our vital functions and reflexes) are almost completely developed and largely responsible for the baby's ability to survive, grow and bond with his carers.

FIGURE 3: The development of the higher brain parts from the lower brain parts

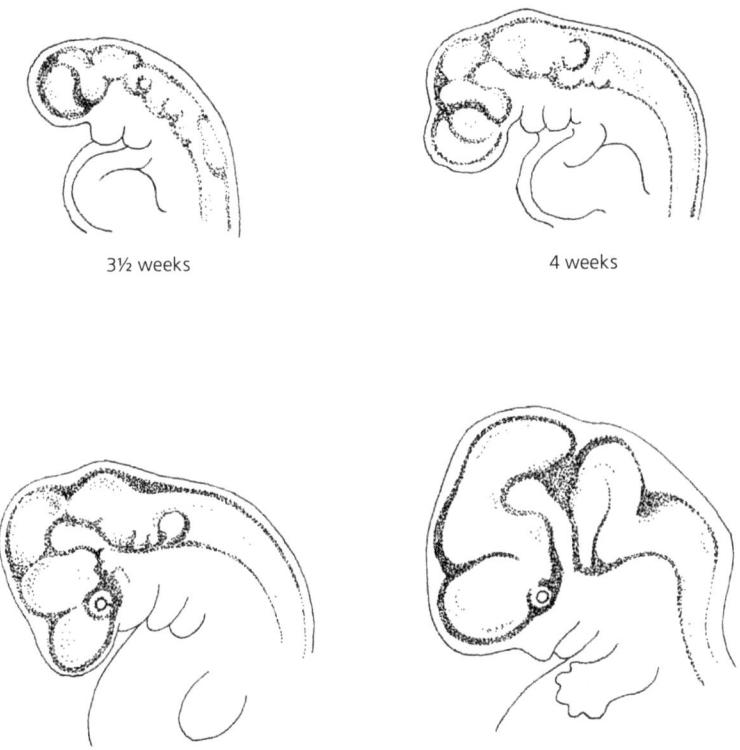

3½ weeks

4 weeks

5⅓ weeks

7 weeks

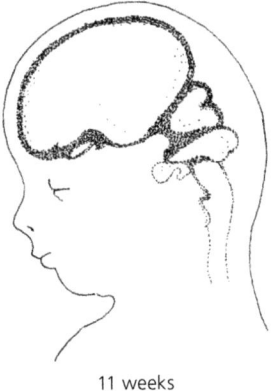

11 weeks

Directly after conception the fertilised cells start to divide, forming a blastosyst. The blastosyst consists of 32 cells, only three to five of which grow into a person – the rest become the placenta. In these three to five cells the complete genetic composition of the person – hair colour, basic personality, body height, eye colour, etc. – is contained.

The nervous system starts developing only 14 days after conception – before the mother is even aware that she is pregnant. During the fifth week after conception, the five brain vesicles ('swellings') are formed, and during the sixth week they start dividing to form the major brain areas and the 12 cranial nerves (the nerve tracts serving the head and face).

The lower, more basic brain parts, which are responsible for reflexes and automatic reactions, are the first to develop, along with some of the sense organs (more about this in chapter 5), forming the basis for the development of the higher brain centra, such as the cortex. If one understands this, the profound effect that sensory development has on the cortex will also be clear. Stimulation of sensory development results in stimulation of various other brain areas, including the cortex, with functions such as cognitive thinking, memory and emotional adjustment. Figure 3 shows how the development of the higher brain parts follows upon the development of the lower parts.

When the foetus is three months old, dramatic growth takes place in the two brain halves (cerebral hemispheres), making them thicker and bulkier. The corpus callosum (a thick band of nerves that connect the two hemispheres) also develops at this stage.

After 24 weeks of pregnancy, your baby could already survive outside the womb. The foetus is now 34 cm long, with the lungs capable of inhaling air and the brain stem regulating rhythmic breathing movements. Although the distinctive sulci (brain fissures) are taking shape in the cerebral cortex, the latter is not yet functional (see figure 4).

FIGURE 4: The sulci of the cerebral cortex

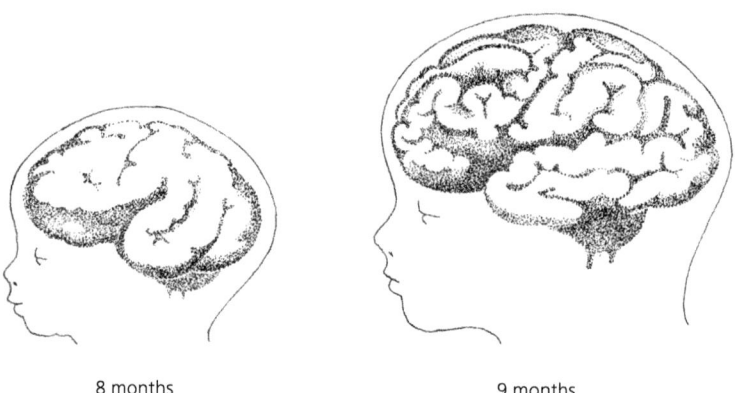

8 months   9 months

Sulci are present in three different sizes: primary, secondary and tertiary. The primary sulci, that start forming at 20 weeks after conception and are completed by seven months after conception, look more or less the same in all humans, while the secondary sulci vary largely from person to person. The tertiary sulci start developing during the last month of pregnancy and continue to grow until around the baby's first birthday. The environment plays a major role during the whole process of sulcus growth.

During the first year of life, the brain becomes more mature, growing to three times its weight at birth. Taking place at molecular level, however, this growth is not as dramatic as the enormous, noticeable growth that happens prenatally.

Prenatal influences on the brain

For as long as we have had to listen to old wives' tales, we have been hearing that a pregnant woman should take care of herself and her baby in order to ensure normal development. Of all the body organs, the central nervous system is probably the most susceptible to prenatal influences. The womb being the highly protective environment that it is, there is actually a lack of stimulation prenatally. Apparently this small, warm, dark and isolated place, which is also much quieter than the external environment, is exactly what the foetus needs for early brain development.

Babies that are born eight or more weeks prematurely, have a high risk of mental and neurological disorders such as visual, auditory or motor disabilities, as well as lack of emotional control, lack of concentration and language handicaps. When these babies are kept in incubators that imitate the conditions inside the womb (i.e. quieter, darker and they are snugly swaddled in special blankets in the foetal position), they are healthier, develop faster and perform better in intelligence tests for babies.

However, most birth defects have no identifiable cause. Known environmental and health factors are responsible for as little as 10 per cent of all defects in babies. So although it is important to take good care of yourself, it is unnecessary to fret and worry about your baby's wellbeing. He is safe and well taken care of in the womb.

The *effect of negative influences* (e.g. medication or alcohol taken by the mother) on brain development is more significant during the first semester of pregnancy, i.e. before all the basic brain structures have developed. After these basic structures have developed and all the neurons have been formed (i.e. after the 18th week after conception) the brain will still be sensitive to potentially harmful influences, albeit to a lesser degree.

The mother's *general health* and her daily calorie intake do not have such a significant effect during the first few months of pregnancy. Notwithstanding the immense development that takes place during this period, the foetus grows very little in size, making it less dependent on the mother's calorie intake. Just as well, as continuous nausea often causes her to eat very little!

Brain development is particularly sensitive to the mother's health and diet. There is a good reason why, in times of famine, pregnant women and children under three years should be given the best nutrition. From halfway through your pregnancy until your child is about two years of age, the growth and development of his brain depends highly upon the quality and quantity of food that he is given. This sensitive period goes hand in hand with the fast growth and development of synapses and dendrites and the myelinisation of nerves. The quality of nutrition during this period has a significant effect on the child's future cognitive, emotional and neurological functions. As this period starts in the womb, and continues during the baby and toddler years, not only does the mother's diet have a significant effect on the baby's brain development, but special attention should also be given to the child's diet during the first two years of his life. Although nutritional deficiencies may be specific, such as an iron or vitamin B deficiency, the most significant effects are due to a general deficiency in the mother's basic diet, like an insufficient calorie intake. Malnutrition can hamper brain development at any stage during the sensitive period. The longer it continues and the earlier in the baby's life it occurs, however, the more serious the effects will be.

Many studies have been conducted regarding the effect of the mother's health and diet on her baby, as well as the role that specific toxins play in the development of certain disorders. Your doctor will be able to give you good advice as to what you should eat, and how much weight you should gain during pregnancy, to ensure that your baby is well nutritioned. The mother's diet plays a more important role in the baby's birth weight than do genetic causes. Malnutrition can lead to low birth weight and size. These babies generally develop more slowly, perform weaker in intelligence tests later in their lives and may even suffer neurological problems.

As the mother's stress levels also affect her unborn baby, enough rest and relaxation are of the utmost importance. Stress hormones that naturally occur in the mother's blood, and are hence transferred to the baby's bloodstream, are a good and normal thing. Normal stress is a healthy part of life. However, if the mother's stress levels are particularly high, due to an extremely stressful period, or a naturally anxious personality for instance, the foetus may receive an overdose of the stress hormones, which can have a negative effect on his development. Studies link stress during pregnancy to miscarriage, low birth weight and premature birth. High stress levels in the mother can also negatively affect brain function, leading to severe tenseness and irritability in the baby. Arrested intellectual and motor development have also been noted.

Do keep in mind, however, that mothers suffering high stress levels and nutritional deficiencies frequently come from a more needy background, smoke and take alcohol or drugs, and often have poor eating habits, making it very difficult to accurately determine the effects of stress. So to be on the safe side, try to remain relatively calm and if you are going through a particularly stressful period, talk to your doctor or therapist and get help of some sort – this is not the time to try and sort out your own problems! It is comforting to know that the placenta serves to break down the mother's stress hormones, safeguarding the foetus against the same intensity of stress. Also, it is more important for the mother to enjoy her pregnancy than to fret about eating the wrong foods or worry about lack of sleep.

So: eat properly, get enough rest, enjoy your pregnancy and trust your body's ability to take care of your baby in the best possible way!

Guidelines for promoting normal development

During the first few months after conception, all the baby needs is the quiet, warm environment of the womb, allowing the mother time to pamper herself, handle her nausea and spoil her hubby before her body becomes too uncomfortable!

The sense of touch is the first to develop, starting shortly after conception. The soft womb is the ideal place for optimal development and there is little that the mother can do to stimulate touch development intrauterally.

The sense of movement also starts developing early. However, the normal activities of the mother and baby offer enough stimulation for optimal development, however.

By the time the baby is born, the sense of smell is already fully developed, allowing him to make smell associations directly after birth. Once again, there is little that the mother can do to stimulate smell prenatally.

The sense of taste also develops early, so that eight weeks after conception the baby can already taste the amniotic fluid, and later on in the pregnancy, also perceive the flavours and aromas that his mother tastes and smells. So although the mother should avoid eating spicy and strongly flavoured foods later in her pregnancy, she should also make a point of exposing her baby to different tastes and flavours.

Later in the pregnancy, the mother can watch her baby's reactions as she experiences different tastes and smells. For instance, the baby often reacts with sudden movements when the mother eats or smells something that he dislikes!

By six months after conception the baby's hearing is already well developed, enabling him to listen, understand sounds and react to a variety of noises. Remember that the mother's body sounds (heartbeat, breathing and intestinal sounds) are much clearer and louder than external sounds. Nevertheless, the baby also hears other sounds and will be more relaxed when exposed to the same ones (songs, music, mother tongue, mother's voice) after his birth that he regularly heard prenatally. A baby will also relax when lying on his mother's stomach, listening to the familiar heartbeat and intestinal sounds that he got used to in the womb.

After five months of pregnancy, you can start talking, singing and playing music to your baby. The more words she hears, the better her language ability. Play music through loudspeakers close to your stomach, watching you baby's reactions. You will notice that, at different times of the day, she reacts differently to various kinds of music. I recommend that you stick to peaceful music – baroque in particular – that produces an alpha rhythm (i.e. the rhythm of a person's brainwaves when he is relaxed but concentrating, as when studying). The largo rhythm, which induces sleep and relaxation, will help you and your baby to relax regularly. Without overdoing it, make music a part of your and your baby's daily routine. It is a good habit that can be continued throughout the baby and childhood years.

During the last month or two of your pregnancy, you can pay attention to the times when your baby is either awake and active, or relaxed inside the womb. Chances are that he is already establishing a routine that can be continued once he is born. When you find that your baby is normally quiet in the mornings, this may mean that after his birth you may have time to take a nap during the morning. Likewise, you can put aside the active times of the day for bathing and playing. Although this is possible, you may also learn for the first time that your scrupulous planning and preparation often do not correspond with that of your baby – and that you have no choice but to adjust your routine to fit in with his!

---

1. L. Eliot, *What's Going On In There?* (New York: Bantam Books, 1999).

5
Sensory development

In the previous chapters we have seen how genes and environment affect your child's brain growth and development, and that the formation of the cerebral cortex largely depends on the electrical activity that takes place in each synapse. Receptors in our sense organs receive information from the environment, which is then transported to the brain via the nerve tracts. With regular stimulation. 'maps' of this information are formed in the brain, enabling us to compare new information with existing information at a later stage. The size of the cortex area allocated to the various body parts is determined by the sensory experiences that that area is exposed to, in other words the amount of stimulation that that brain area receives. Experience, i.e. stimulation, affects these 'brain maps' *throughout our lives*, and not only during the first months of our lives.

Efficient adaptation to the environment, or appropriate reactions, depends on a person's sensory-motor level. Old people often have a limited ability to move and adapt because their sensory systems (sense organs) have become less efficient. Their typical walking pattern is usually the result of poor functioning of the sensory systems registering the movement of body parts, touch or balance. When this faulty information from the sense organs reaches the brain, it results in a maladjustment, for example, poor balance. Maladjustment can also be the result of poor integration among the various sensory systems.

FIGURE 5: Model of sensory integration

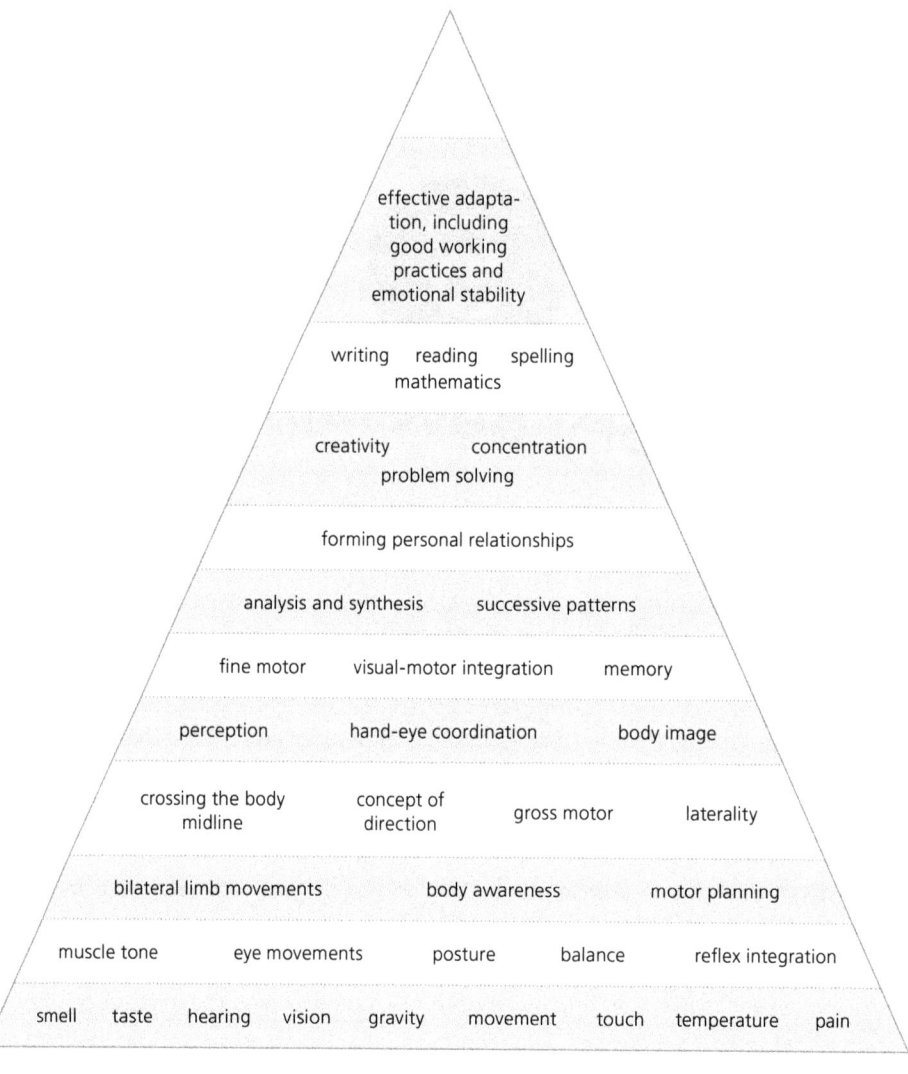

(adapted from research by A. Jean Ayres)

In a young child the sensory systems are still developing and integrating. The child needs practice in order to manage efficient collaboration of all the systems. Poor integration of sensations in the child leads to inappropriate reactions and movement patterns. Look at a baby who takes his first steps: The input from the muscles and joints is obviously not enough to ensure good balance. If efficient integration of the various sensory systems takes place (the child's balance and gait improve), further learning can happen effectively; if not, the result is a faulty learning process (poor balance).

Figure 5 shows the different stages at which the development of sensory systems takes place. The sense organs are along the bottom of the triangle, forming the basis for development. In this model, development begins at the base of the triangle, moving higher up as the child gets older. Like bricks in a wall, skills higher up in the triangle are built upon skills at the base of the triangle. And as with a building, weak building blocks or skills at the base or foundation, result in a weak wall or skills higher up. So if the child has a problem integrating the basic sensory systems (sense organs), he will most likely also have a problem with something like balance or body image, and probably with social skills and handwriting as well. Sensory development starts immediately after conception and long before the baby is born.

Both the child's genetic composition and his environment play a role in the formation and development of his brain. Although developmental handicaps in children can be either physical or genetic in origin, they can often be prevented by efficient stimulation of the young child. The best way to notice a lag is to know your child and to spend plenty of time with him. That way you will know what he can and cannot do, what he enjoys, what he finds hard and what role his own personality plays in his daily routine. If a lag is suspected, professional advice should be sought without delay. The sooner a potential problem is detected, the sooner it can be solved or the smaller its effect will be on the child's functioning.

Sense of touch

Touch is the first functional system in the womb, affording us our first perceptions of this world. It is through touch that we are fed and pacified and that we form our first bond with another human being. Touch is the primary system of contact with the external world. Before the language, motor and cognitive abilities develop to guide us in experiences and interactions with the environment, we are highly dependent on touch.

Although all forms of sensory input are important for optimal development, in the foetus and young baby, touch plays a particularly important part in the quality of brain development. During the first weeks after birth, touch and motor activity are the most significant active brain areas. Touch includes the sensations of light touch (coarse and soft textures), deep pressure, temperature, pain and vibration on the skin surface. Increasing the variety of touch sensations in the baby will also promote various other aspects of brain and cognitive development.

An interesting aspect is that although babies can experience pain from an early age, they do not psychologically associate pain with suffering and so do not cognitively realise that they are in pain. As the baby does not have a conscious memory, he will probably not remember the pain. However, at an unconscious level, repeated painful experiences may well have a more lasting effect. The fact that a baby cannot experience or remember pain the way that we do, may be a consolation to parents whose baby has to undergo painful procedures in hospital.

As a young baby cannot compensate for low, and especially very high, temperatures, his environmental temperature should be regulated by means of clothing, blankets, coolers or heaters, according to the circumstances.

Touch and physical contact is vital for the baby's sensory and motor development, as well as for his physical growth, emotional wellbeing, cognitive development and general health. Studies have shown that physical handling of a baby animal during the first 10 days after its birth permanently reduces the stress response, helping it to recover more quickly after a stressful incident. Another study with animals has shown that when a mother and baby are separated at birth, the baby may suffer a weakened immune system up until the age of six years.

As touch stimulates the young baby's brain more than any of the other senses, it is probably the best, and also one of the easiest, ways to shape and ensure the child's emotional and intellectual wellbeing. There are many different types of touch stimuli, each of which is perceived by different receptors and transported by different tracts to areas in the brain. The baby experiences the different types of touch as follows:

- **light touch:** the loose-fitting clothes that he wears on his body
- **heavy pressure:** when something heavy (e.g. a heavy blanket) rests on him and when he is held and cuddled
- **differences in temperature:** the temperature inside and outside the room; the mother's cold hands and the lukewarm bath water
- **movement on the skin:** stroking or massaging
- **recognising objects with different textures:** coarse and smooth textures touching the skin

Although it could be regarded by some as boring academic information, it is interesting to take note of the different brain areas which are employed during the learning process. All these brain areas are stimulated by touch impulses, among others.

1. The reticular formation determines the state of alertness, affecting a person's concentration. When you feel drowsy or sleepy, as when you are listening to a boring speech, it is the result of the reticular formation acting like a sieve, filtering the

stimuli from the environment and allowing very little to pass through, causing you to fall asleep. When a loud noise wakes you up, it is the result of an auditory impulse travelling from your ears to the reticular formation, changing your state of alertness.

2. The motor planning area is responsible for the efficient mastering and execution of motor actions. Before you hit a ball with a racket, for instance, this area plans the movement and sends all the necessary impulses to muscles and joints, ensuring that the movement is properly executed. Not only sporty movements, but also tasks like climbing stairs, brushing teeth, skipping and functional tasks such as making tea and laying a tray, are involved. Poor motor planning results in clumsiness and poor coordination of movements.

3. The area for the manipulation of objects enables a person to feel what it is that he or she is holding, and what the object looks like. When you pick up a pencil and start writing, you do not need to look at the pencil, as all the information is supplied by the area for the manipulation of objects, freeing your eyes to look at the page on which you are writing. Fine coordination is closely connected with this area. Tasks such as writing, stringing beads, glueing and cutting are dependent on the efficient manipulation of objects.

4. The limbic system is closely connected with emotional adjustment. This area greatly affects various other brain areas, playing an important role in a person's total functioning. Touch stimulation has a noticeable effect on the limbic system, which is why, when you are emotionally upset, it usually helps to be held tightly or hugged by the right person. The touch stimulation (hug) physically affects the limbic system, making you feel better emotionally.

The above brain areas are the principal areas affected and stimulated by touch stimuli (other areas affected by touch are not discussed here). Therefore, when playing games that are specifically aimed at stimulating your child's touch organs, these areas will also be stimulated.

Children with *dysfunctional touch integration* may react in some of the following ways:

- Refusal to touch certain textures, such as finger paint, play dough or sand
- Kicking off their blankets at night, even when it is cold
- Constantly taking off their clothes and disliking jerseys, for instance
- Refusal to take off their clothes and wearing only certain garments or textures
- Refusal to wear shoes or refusal to walk barefoot
- Fussiness with food, especially regarding the textures of some foods
- Refusal to wash their face and hair
- Hurting and crying easily, or not feeling hurt and sustaining bruises inadvertently
- Accepting hugs and kisses selectively

There are various games that parents can play with their child in order to stimulate touch and promote integration. Most are games that parents like to play with their baby or child anyway – a natural urge that probably exists for the child's good! Games should induce enjoyment and good parent-child interaction. If the child is scared or reacts negatively, the game should be adapted to suit his needs. If he repeatedly refuses to take part or continually reacts negatively, however, professional advice must be sought. Here are some games to enjoy with your child:

1. Crawling, rolling and gliding are all actions that stimulate touch and promote integration. Lay your young baby down on different textures that he can feel, lie upon and roll over on. An older baby or young child can roll or glide on different textures, for example, blankets or towels covering a slide or a slope made of mats or thin mattresses. Use materials with different textures, like rubber, wool, foam rubber, leather, silky fabric and coarse fabric. Fantasy will enhance the fun factor. Say something like, "I'm a big lion and I'm going to catch you!" before 'chasing' him across the textures. Imitate animal movements such as a slithering snake, a rolling dog and a fish in the water. Let your child wear only the basic clothing, exposing large parts of his skin to the different textures.
2. Open a cardboard box on both sides. The child lies inside the box, rolling over and over in a specific direction. Use your imagination to make fantasy part of the game – imagine the child is the wheel of a big truck or a tumble dryer going around and around. Put large beads or sponge balls at one point, where the child picks them up before rolling to another point and dropping them into a container. Older children can pick up jigsaw puzzle pieces before rolling to the second point, where the puzzle is then put together. Sometimes just rolling around can be huge fun, especially if you have a large lawn or plenty of blankets.
3. Imagine the child is riding in a boat. He lies on his back or stomach on an old blanket, towel or duvet (alternate the textures), holding onto the blanket as the parent pulls him along a slippery floor. Going around corners will increase stimulation as the child rolls from side to side – just beware of sharp edges! This is great fun – enjoy it with your child.
4. Imagine the child is a piece of dough that has to be rolled out for making biscuits. The child lies on the carpet while the parent uses a big ball as 'rolling pin', pressing fairly hard and rolling it over his arms, legs and body. The deep pressure sensation is usually relaxing, making this a suitable activity before bedtime. Talking in a soft, low voice and using dimmed lighting together with soft, peaceful music will add to the calming atmosphere. The child soon relaxes and may even fall asleep! If he wants you to repeat the rolling, press harder on the ball, but not so hard that you hurt his back. Naming the body parts as you roll over them will also teach the child their names. By about four years of age you can start teaching 'left' and 'right' as you roll the ball over the relevant sides.

5. The 'hotdog' game is very popular, so be prepared to play it over and over again! Lay the child down on a large blanket on the floor, then wrap him in the blanket, leaving his head uncovered if he feels unsafe. The child is now a 'hotdog' to which you add 'butter', 'tomato sauce' and all sorts of 'condiments' by rubbing your hands over the blanket, applying a fair amount of pressure. Unroll your child by pulling on one side of the blanket, allowing him to roll out at a speed that he enjoys (it shouldn't scare him or make him feel uncomfortable).
6. Using chalk, draw a picture on a textured surface – a piece of mat or even cardboard – which the child then erases with his hands, feet or forearms. The child is then given a turn to make his own drawing or scribbling, which he also erases.
7. Using soft chalk, make spots on the child's body, which he then removes with differently textured materials such as a ball of wool, a scourer sponge, a towel, a piece of mat and a bath sponge. This can also be done in the bath using finger paint or coloured body paint soap, naming the body parts as they are marked and erased, as well as the colours that are used.

The following is a summary of the advantages that stimulation of the touch system has for a child:

- It is vital for the sensory-motor development of a baby.
- It is important for physical growth and development.
- It has a positive effect on the baby's emotional wellbeing.
- It promotes cognitive development.
- It promotes the baby's general health.
- It can reduce stress levels in the baby.

Children thrive on touch and physical contact, especially during the first few months of their lives. In my therapy sessions, I have seen enormous emotional and intellectual growth, as well as behaviour normalisation and improved concentration, after stimulation of the touch system in particular, not only in babies, but also in primary school children and, in some special cases, even in grown-ups.

Vestibular sense (sense of movement)

Although we seldom think of the experience of movement as a sense, that is in fact exactly what it is. The experience of movement is the sensation that you feel when you close your eyes in a moving vehicle. You can feel when the car slows down or speeds up, turns left or right, whether a corner is sharp or long and whether you are moving uphill or downhill. These sensations are received by different receptors, such as those in the inner ear, stomach, weight-carrying joints, muscles and eyes. From there the messages are sent to the relevant brain areas, where all the messages are processed (integrated). You then perceive the sensation of movement.

The vestibular sense is vital for normal and optimal development in a baby. The baby is born with a well-developed vestibular system, which is critical for early brain development, especially at an unconscious, subcortical level. Efficient development of this system is vital for the development of the head control and body posture necessary for the movement of various body parts, and initially, the eyes in particular. The development of balance and the concept of left and right are also built upon the proper functioning of the vestibular system.

Although the vestibular system and hearing system start developing at the same time and both are differentiated by five weeks after conception, the vestibular system develops faster and reaches its full size and shape by five months after conception. By this time, the nerve tracts to the eyes and spinal cord have also started to myelinise. The vestibular system is particularly vulnerable during the prenatal stage, when it can be affected by infections, low birth weight, hereditary factors and thyroid disorders.

A well-developed vestibular sense enables the unborn baby to orientate himself so that, towards the end of the pregnancy, he can turn himself in the optimal position to be born. If, for some reason, the vestibular system has not developed optimally or reached maturity, the chances of your baby being in the breech position at the end of the pregnancy are increased. This system is responsible for the development of the various reflexes that are present at birth and which will be tested by your doctor as soon as the baby is born.

The vestibular sense, which is vital for the development of balance, continues to develop until at least the age of seven years, and presumably even until the child has finished growing. This gradual development after birth is necessary in order to accommodate the greater scope of movement and growth in the baby and child, and leads to particularly slow myelinisation of some of the vestibular nerve tracts.

The advantages of vestibular stimulation are far more important for intellectual and neurological development than was ever realised in the past. A child who is rocked, swayed, generally handled and carried around frequently, receives plenty of vestibular stimulation, which directly affects the sensations of balance and movement, and forms an important part of the baby's earliest sensory experiences. It also plays a critical part in the organisation of other sensory and motor modalities, including the higher emotional and cognitive abilities.

There is ample evidence that extra vestibular stimulation can improve a baby's brain and intellectual abilities. Vestibular stimulation is generally good for young babies, while babies who are pacified by means of vestibular stimulation, are also more alert, resulting in better development in various spheres. Premature babies thrive with stimulation of the vestibular system, and as one of the baby's best developed senses, it also allows easy access for the stimulation and development of the rest of the brain.

Movement patterns form the basis of learning, while different levels of movement stimulate development. The impulses (input) for vestibular-proprioceptive functions come from the muscles, joints and inner ear. Different movements executed against gravity stimulate the semicircular canals of the inner ear in particular. When, during movement the head is held in different planes against gravity, all three canals are stimulated. This happens when the child swings or crawls in the stomach position, swings or spins in the sitting position, and swings in the back position (e.g. the hammer and nail game where two adults swing the child by his arms and legs). During each of these three positions, the child's head is in a different position with regard to the earth's gravity, each stimulating a different semicircular canal.

Children with repeated ear infections whose movement is somehow restricted, do not develop according to expectation, and are often either scared of movement or are rough and cannot get enough movement. Through movement, a child also learns more about his own body and motor abilities, resulting in the development of his self-image and body image.

A child that never crawls, for instance, firstly misses out on learning an important movement pattern (left leg and right arm moving simultaneously, i.e. contralateral movement), secondly, does not carry weight on his shoulders/hands and hips/knees for long enough periods (negatively affecting balance and even pencil grip), and thirdly does not get enough movement with his head at a 30-degree angle with regard to the earth's gravity (stimulating the horisontal semicircular canal), resulting in possible lags. No lag can, however, be predicted, and many people go through life completely normal without ever having crawled.

Developmental lags in the vestibular system may be suspected if some of the following reactions are present in a child:

- Avoids running and jumping games
- Avoids climbing frames, is often scared (and his dad, particularly, fears that he will become a sissy)
- Only uses swings with which he is familiar
- Avoids, or is scared of, a merry-go-round
- Gets hurt easily, refusing further participation in movement games
- Takes part in all games, but in a headlong manner, leading to injuries
- Often appears clumsy
- Often falls and appears uncomfortable when running
- Dislikes games that involve being thrown up into the air

Games that stimulate the vestibular sense include lots of movement, with the child in different positions. Here are some examples of games that you can play with your child:

1. Use a large, inflated tube, such as a tractor tube. (Children love playing on these, so do make an effort to get hold of one – they are suitable for inside or outside play.) Sitting on the tube, both feet to the outside, the child tries to bounce up and down 10 times without falling off. Older children can try to move sideways in a circle while bouncing. Jumping on a trampoline will also practise this up-and-down movement.
2. Imagine the child is flying in a helicopter. Lying in the stomach position on a small blanket on a slippery floor, he uses his hands and feet to push on the floor in an effort to spin himself around. A baby can be assisted by you pulling and turning the blanket, while an older child must be encouraged to do it himself in order to exercise the arm movements and shoulder muscles as well.
3. The child lies on her stomach in a hammock or in a parent-held towel, while being swayed in different directions. A towel allows for varied directions of movement – forwards, backwards, sideways, diagonal and circular. Just be sure to remain upright, or you may be stuck with back pain! For an older child the two parents hold the towel on either side. When using a hammock, a length of rope or elastic can be attached to the wall, allowing the child to pull and sway herself.
4. The child lies on his stomach over a large ball (not so large that the child is scared by its height – he must be able to press his hands on the floor with reasonable ease). He now puts his hands on the floor, carrying weight on his arms and shoulders. If the child is scared, hold him by the hips, ensuring that he still carries weight on his arms and that his head is lower than his feet and hips. The idea is that the child rolls forward and backward with his head down – also known as the inverse position. (If you do not have a large ball, a rolled-up mattress or firm mat can also be used.)
5. Imagine the child is riding in a cable car. Using a blanket on a slippery floor, the child lies in the back position with his legs pulled up, using both hands to hold onto a short broomstick held in the parent's hands (or he holds directly onto the parent's hands). The parent pulls the child around the floor while he holds on, trying to lift his head and keeping his legs pulled up. Over and above the stimulation that he gets from the movement, it is also excellent exercise for numerous muscle groups in the child's shoulders and torso.
6. Use a big, sturdy ball – a soccer ball will do nicely. Standing with her back towards a target (a circle on the wall or a basket lying on its side), the child rolls the ball between her legs towards the target. The parent rolls the ball back between the child's legs, or the child fetches it herself. Crumpled-up paper balls, rolled-up socks or soft toys can also be used. Make sure that the child regularly lifts up her head, as dizziness can occur when the head is held down for too long. Moving the head up and down in this manner provides excellent movement stimulation.
7. The child turns around and around in the standing position until the parent gives the signal to stop (e.g. says, "stop" or stops the music that is playing). He then turns in the opposite direction, repeating the game for as long as he enjoys it. Stop the game when the

child looks pale or starts looking or feeling dizzy. The child can also turn while moving in a certain direction, for instance, into his father's arms, and then back in the opposite direction, into his mother's arms. It is important to observe your child's reactions throughout to ensure that there is not excessive movement as this may lead to nausea. If your child feels nauseous or dizzy, let him lie down on his back with an ice cube in each hand.

The advantages of stimulating the vestibulary sense can be summarised as follows:

- It is vital for the baby's intellectual and neurological development.
- The sensations of balance and movement play an important role in various everyday activities.
- It plays a critical part in the organisation of other sensory and motor functions, affecting the higher emotional and cognitive functions.
- It is beneficial to the general development of the young foetus.
- Babies who are pacified through movement sensations are visually more alert.
- Continuous, repeated vestibular stimulation, such as slow rocking movements, can reduce the baby's level of alertness (making him more sleepy).
- Fast successive, arrhythmic movements can increase the baby's level of alertness, causing anxiety.
- Premature babies thrive with extra vestibular stimulation.
- As one of the newborn baby's best developed senses, it allows easy access for the stimulation of the developing brain, promoting optimal brain development.

Sense of smell

Smell plays a much more important role in our daily lives than is generally assumed, being involved with social interaction, sexual attraction and parent-child bonding, as well as with our appetites, of course! Smell is transported from the nose to the relevant brain area via direct nerve tracts, following a short and direct path to conscious smell sensation.

By the time a baby is born, the sense of smell is relatively mature and well developed. It is unique in the sense that new cells are formed right through our lives. Old cells die off and are replaced as often as every 60 days. The quality of the new cells depends on the health of their predecessors. General cell quality starts diminishing during mid-childhood, being negatively affected by factors such as infections, cigarette smoke, pollution and environmental toxins.

At birth, the olfactory (smell) tracts are already fully myelinised, allowing optimal development to take place inside the womb. As the foetus perceives the same flavours and aromas as the mother, the baby starts perceiving the environment through this sense long before he is born!

A newborn baby reacts noticeably to the smell of amniotic fluid. His reactions to different smells normally vary from sucking and crying to a change in his tempo of breathing. He quickly gets accustomed to new flavours, however, when he is continually or regularly exposed to these. Girls are generally more sensitive to flavours and aromas than boys.

The sense of smell plays a key role in the baby's earliest emotional development, being instrumental in the formation of his first emotional bond with his mother and other significant people in his life. Young babies find it comforting to be surrounded by their own smell, e.g. the smell of their own bodies and saliva, so do not be too hasty in replacing clothing or burp cloths with clean ones smelling of soap! Young babies often get attached to their own blankets and soft toys because of the comforting smell. They also quickly get accustomed to the smell of their siblings, soon learning to recognise them through their sense of smell.

So we see that many of a baby's first impressions of the world, in the womb as well in the first few months of his life, are perceived by his sense of smell.

Note: Do not expose your child to excessively strong fragrances or to too many different fragrances at a time, as strong and/or mixed fragrances can cause headaches or nausea in a child. Prevent overstimulation by limiting the number of fragrances at any specific time.

Sense of taste

The sense of taste develops very early, so that when a baby is born, he already shows a preference for pleasant tastes and a noticeable dislike for unpleasant tastes. Taste also plays an important role in the exploration of his environment. The taste sensations are registered in the brain, affecting various reflexes with regard to feeding, such as saliva secretion, the swallow reflex and tongue movements. The taste impulses are also transported to brain parts related to the emotional aspects of feeding, as in the motivation to eat and drink, and the joy derived from eating and drinking. The taste sensation is further registered in the cortex, where it is perceived consciously.

The first taste organs develop only eight weeks after conception and continue to increase until after the baby is born. Chemicals in the amniotic fluid stimulate the taste organs, resulting in a prenatal taste experience that affects the baby's food preferences at birth. While a newborn baby is only interested in sweet tastes, he is able to distinguish between different types of sugar and different concentrations of a sugar solution. Sour and bitter tastes normally cause strong reactions in a newborn baby, while salt, although it can be tasted, does not evoke the same level of response.

The experience of taste plays an important role in a baby's emotional development. A sweet, fatty taste (such as breastmilk) affects his state of mind, pacifying the baby, increasing his attention span or helping him to fall asleep.

Although smell and taste are normally stimulated throughout the day, extra care can be taken to ensure that your baby is optimally stimulated in this regard. Here are a few games that can be used for stimulating the senses of smell and taste:

1. Divide ready-made or home-made play dough into pieces, adding a different food flavouring to each. Playing with the dough will expose the child to the flavours. You will be amazed to see how much interest a baby of only a few months old shows in the different flavours.
2. Use hand creams, bath oils and body powders with different fragrances, naming and discussing the fragrances with an older child. Also encourage your child to smell your perfume and deodorant.
3. During meals, name and discuss the different smells and tastes of the foods. Play guessing games while preparing the food, encouraging the child to guess what is being cooked, whether you are baking dessert, or whether there is meat or fish in the pan.
4. Guessing games can also be played during the meal. The child must close his eyes and guess what food you put in his mouth, employing the taste, smell and touch senses in the mouth to find the answer. Remember to alternate the guessing games by also giving the parent a turn to do the guessing, otherwise the child may get bored.
5. Wash toys, especially soft toys, with differently fragranced soaps or bath foams. If the child is helping, you can pour the fragrance into the water, otherwise you can just apply some to the toy to add a smell after it has dried.
6. Fill soft 'balls' with herbs, giving each of them a different fragrances. (Old socks work well.) Encourage your baby or child to play with the balls.
7. Tie soft toys or clothes in a plastic bag together with fresh or dried herbs, leaving them for a few hours for the fragrance to be infused.
8. A young child uses his mouth to explore objects, gathering information about their texture, temperature, taste and smell by sticking them into his mouth. Allow him to explore things in this manner – it is only in the baby years that this is acceptable, so do not deny him the opportunity! If this way of exploring objects does not subside spontaneously, or if your baby does not explore objects with his mouth at all, it is advisable to consult an occupational therapist.

Sense of vision

Although the visual brain and the experience of vision are relatively primitive when a baby is born, he can recognise his mother's face only hours after his birth! By the time he is six months old, all the primary visual abilities have started to develop. Having received no stimulation at all in the dark, protective womb, visual experiences and stimulation are vital for normal and efficient development of the nerve tracts that register vision.

The first visual tissue starts developing only 22 days after conception, however, after this, visual development takes place in two phases. The first phase is genetically controlled, while the second is controlled by the experiences and stimulation that the baby receives when seeing objects in his environment. Early stimulation and experiences are critical for the formation of the baby's brain, enabling him to correctly perceive the environment later, in order to ensure efficient development of his visual-perceptual functions. If these functions do not develop completely, the child may experience reading and/or spelling problems later on.

The development of hand-eye coordination, which affects functions such as ball play and handwriting, is also affected by a baby's early visual experiences. The more the baby sees in accordance with his level of vision at a certain age, the better his chances later in life of performing well in those tasks and abilities which are dependent on vision.

By the time the baby is about two months old, the cortex starts taking over most of the visual tasks from the subcortical sections of the brain. Vision then becomes a conscious sensation to which the baby also begins to react consciously, recognising people and smiling at them. Between the second and eighth months of the baby's life, the number of synapses in the brain's visual cortex suddenly explodes, resulting in a rapid improvement of his visual ability until his first birthday, by which time it is almost at the same level as that of an adult. By the age of four months the areas in the visual cortex that identify colour, as well as the baby's ability to see with both eyes at the same time, enabling him to perceive depth and dimension, are fully developed.

After a baby is born, his vision develops rapidly, soon becoming the main sense that children use for learning about people and the world. A child's brain and intellect are shaped and developed by the types of visual experiences and visual-motor activities that he is exposed to early in his life.

During every waking moment a baby's eyes are open, enabling him to receive visual impulses. The parent can add interest to this visual world by alternating the environment or objects in the environment. By talking about the objects, allowing him to touch them and adding movement to them, you also involve other senses, promoting natural integration of the senses. You can, for example, move a toy that makes a specific sound in front of your baby, or you can say the name of the toy, or sing as you move it. You can allow the toy to touch your baby, or you can let him hold and feel it. Or put the toy down, rocking or swaying your baby closer and further away from it while you sing or talk.

Although vision in itself is important, eye movements are vital for efficient eye control. The eyes can follow a moving object or be kept still, focusing on a specific object. Without efficient and controlled eye movements, reading for instance, will be almost impossible. The eye muscles responsible for the movement of the eyes are skeleton muscles, working according to the same principles as any other skeleton muscle responsible for the movement of a body part or limb. Eye muscles can be strengthened to promote more efficient eye movements, gaining better eye control.

Here are some activities that you can use to promote good eye control in your child from a young age:

1. Hold an interesting object, like a small toy or finger puppet, in front of your baby, encouraging him to follow it with his eyes. Move it in all directions, i.e. up, down, left, right, diagonally and in a circle. A young baby will only be able to follow large objects, but as he gets older, smaller objects can be used. Initially he will move his head as well, but by the age of five years he should be able to follow objects using eye movements only.
2. Putting pictures inside your baby's cot, within his field of vision will give him something to look at when he is awake. Start with large black and white shapes only, making them more complex and colourful as the baby gets older. Alternate pictures daily.
3. Any ball game will encourage eye movements. Poor ball skills are often the result of an inability to follow the ball with the eyes. Use a big ball with your young baby, making them smaller as he gets older and his skills improve.
4. Hand or finger puppets combined with interesting movements and/or stories will keep a child's imagination captured for quite a while.
5. Using a small torch (or holding a piece of cardboard with a small hole over the light of a larger torch), move its light around a dark room. Focus the light on familiar objects in the room, encouraging the child to follow the light with his eyes.
6. Put a sticker (preferably a face or animal that the child can 'talk' to) on your child's finger, then ask him to make the figure perform different actions, such as dancing, singing, climbing up high, bending down low. Following the sticker with his eyes will also teach the child the basic spatial concepts.
7. Partially hiding behind a screen or piece of furniture, hold a soft toy in your hand, letting it 'jump out' in a different place each time. The child must try to spot it in the shortest possible time. If there are two or more children, they can try to spot the toy first – using more than one toy will add to the fun.
8. Holding your young child in your arms, slowly move him around while he looks at a target (his other parent, a friend, a toy, the television). This encourages him to fix his eyes on a person or object while his body is being swayed and turned.
9. Pull the child on a sheet of cardboard or push him in his stroller, encouraging him to pick up objects such as balls, beanbags and soft toys as he passes them. This action of watching the 'target', judging distance and seizing accurately requires eye fixation during movement.

Colour is not just something that we perceive visually. According to colour therapists, it can also be used as a barometer with regard to our moods and feelings. Not only do we choose colours to match our mood, but our mood can also be influenced and changed by colours. Eight colours, each with its own light frequency or vibration, have a physical effect on human beings.

Colour therapists even use colour to accelerate the healing process by focusing different colours of light on different body parts. In the Western world, we are inclined to choose colours for interior decorating without realising that we prefer certain colours because of the way they make us feel! We form emotional associations with certain colours that we relate to specific events. Some colours are also related to symbolic or religious events or rituals.

Colours can be divided into 'work' colours, such as the reds, yellows and oranges, and 'feel' colours, such as the blues and purples. Kitchens and other 'busy' rooms in the house, such as a playroom, can be painted in bright colours to encourage movement and activity.

The role that colour plays in a room should not be disdained. Light can affect the perception of colour by means of shadows and light spots, changing the complete ambience of a room. Colour is a live medium that can, together with light, alter a person's mood. Keep that in mind the next time that your baby or child is in an impossible mood. You may change his mood by taking him outside to play on the lawn, or taking him into a blue-painted room, drawing the curtains to dim the light and create a softer, more peaceful atmosphere.

Although people react differently to colours, there are some general guidelines that apply to most people. You should be aware of the effect that light and colour have on your own, as well as your baby's, mood.

- **Red** is a strong primary colour that radiates energy, vitality, power and vigour, suitable for countering low blood pressure, low energy levels and drowsiness, and providing more 'vooma'.
- **Black**, being composed of all the colours, suggests depth. It represents humility and negativity, but also knowledge and science as well as attractiveness. Black is not used in colour therapy.
- **Green** is the colour of nature, representing harmony, balance and neutrality.
- **Blue** represents the sea and air and is a receding colour associated with tranquility, relaxation and peace. It is used in the treatment of high blood pressure, asthma and migraines.
- **Purple** is a spiritual colour representing honour, values and hope. It is used for countering feelings of hopelessness and low self-esteem, contributing to strengthen a person's personality.
- **White** reflects all the colours and represents innocence, isolation and wisdom. As a neutral colour it constitutes transparency and truth.
- **Yellow** is the colour closest to light, representing the intellect, thought and criticism. It is applied in the relief of rheumatoid arthritis.
- **Grey** is a colour that actually denies its status as a colour! It depicts service and purposefulness.

- **Brown** is the colour of earth and death. Sacrifice, purposefulness and determination are associated with brown.

Colour is an interesting aspect of visual perception that should not be disregarded. However, with intensity, personal differences and association playing such a significant role, the use of colour cannot be applied slavishly.

Sense of hearing

The hearing sense develops early and matures gradually, continually adapting to the child's experience. By the third trimester of pregnancy the unborn baby starts to listen to and understand sounds. Early experience through language and music is vital for the stimulation and development of the higher aspects of brain functioning.

Ten to 20 weeks after conception, 16 000 hair cells have already developed in the foetus' ear. By 23 weeks after conception, he can react to sound, and by the sixth month of pregnancy he can react to a variety of sounds. Because the unborn baby is mostly exposed to the mother's body sounds, a newborn baby can often be pacified by putting him on his mother's stomach, where he can hear her heartbeat, intestinal sounds, and so forth. The unborn baby can also listen to music played through loudspeakers near the pregnant mother's stomach. As the type of music has an effect on the baby's development, it is recommended that you make a study of this instead of just letting your baby listen to any kind of music.

The sounds that an unborn baby hears, are the beginning of his language development and also affect his intellectual development. Babies as young as four days old react positively on hearing their mother tongue and are more restless when exposed to a foreign language. Every subtle aspect of the sounds that a baby hears has an effect on the development of his hearing sense.

During the preschool and first school years, hearing is flexible and adaptable. The critical period for optimal stimulation of the simpler aspects of hearing development ends earlier than that of the more complex aspects of hearing. Language and music stimulate intellectual and emotional development in a baby and child, music being a particularly efficient way of developing the baby's simple thinking patterns into more complex patterns. His brain already recognises the key, expression and tempo of music, using the same system for music interpretation as for the interpretation of perception, memory and language. Children who are exposed to music often perform better in motor tasks, mathematics and reading. The younger a child is when he learns to play a musical instrument, the larger the brain area that is used for playing the instrument. According to studies, the spatial reasoning ability of preschool children who took singing or piano lessons, showed a noticeable improvement within eight months.[1]

The importance of talking to a baby in order to develop his language ability cannot be overemphasised. The more words the child hears, the better his vocabulary and language ability will eventually become. Leaving a baby in the care of someone who uses limited (or a foreign) language, negatively affects the child's ultimate mother tongue ability.

Apart from the auditory impulses that your baby receives during his daily routine, the following games can be used for optimal stimulation of the hearing sense:

1. It is important for a young baby to experience a sense of being listened to. Make eye contact with your baby, encouraging him to make more sounds, and later on practise words.
2. Encourage auditory memory by giving your child instructions to carry out. Start off with one-step instructions, gradually increasing the number of steps as he gets older. "Give me your hand", is an example of a one-step instruction. This can be extended to something like, "Take the spoon, put it on the table and call Daddy," which would be a three-step instruction suitable for a much older child.
3. In a quiet moment, listen with your child to how many different sounds you can hear, such as the humming of the refrigerator, a door that opens and a bird that sings.
4. Begin with auditory associations, e.g. "What different things can we do with our eyes/hands/feet?" Also talk about things that one sees during daytime or nighttime, e.g. the sun, mountains and birds during the day, and the moon, stars and owls in the evening.
5. Teach your child simple nursery rhymes and songs. Although a baby can obviously not join in, he will be stimulated by the sounds, sequence, rhyme and different inflections of your voice. When he grows a little older, he may only repeat the last word with you. Still later, his memory will be better, and before you know it, your child will be saying and singing numerous nursery rhymes and songs.
6. Silly sentences can be great fun with a somewhat older child who has developed a fair vocabulary. Say one of the following, which the child must then repeat and correct:

You comb your teeth.
I eat my porridge with a spade.
Annie drank the cake.
Johnny wears a pretty dress.
I catch the ball with my nose.
The telephone is running.
The cat has soft feathers.
I smell with my ears.
I sleep in my fridge.
I draw with a broom.

Give the older child a turn to make his own silly sentences, which the parent then corrects.
7. Opposites can be used from a young age by pointing out differences at first (high/low; fat/thin; short/long). Later the child can be asked to:
   - correct sentences – The fridge is shorter than the pencil.
   - fill in opposites – If the boy is not fat, he is …
   - point out and name opposites in picture books.
8. Sorting sounds can also become a fun game. Think of loud and soft sounds. Which sounds are important (e.g. doorbell) and which are unimportant (e.g. humming of refrigerator)?

It is important to extend your child's vocabulary by continually exposing him to new words and encouraging him to use them. Talk to your baby or toddler a lot and encourage him to talk to you too. Start reading to him at an early age. Not only does reading extend his vocabulary, but it encourages the baby to listen and the toddler to visualise. He also discovers that there is a fascinating world hidden inside books, cultivating in him a love of reading.

Music is a powerful and particularly efficient way to stimulate a child, improving his concentration, reflexes, listening skills and emotional development. As babies recognise music that they have heard in the womb, a mother can introduce her baby to the wonderful world of music even before he is born, and especially during the last trimester of her pregnancy. Peaceful, soothing music is always a good idea, as loud sounds may scare or frighten the baby. Baroque music, with its slow tempo, and focusing mainly on the alpha rhythm, is a good choice for your unborn baby. Mozart's *'Eine kleine Nachtmusik'* is a good example. Play your choice of baroque music to your unborn baby daily, noting his movements – you will soon discover whether he likes the music or not!

As with other sensory stimulation, music assists and reinforces the 'wiring' (i.e. the formation and establishment of dendrites) in your baby's brain. Because music is a universal language and the baby already recognises his mother's voice, a mother can also sing to her unborn baby. Music with fairly high notes has a calming effect on babies.

It is important that your baby should listen to music every day. Continue to play choir, piano and violin music, as in Mozart's and Beethoven's concertos. Do not just play it, but also offer it in an organised way, ensuring that your baby gets the most out of your effort. Choose the baroque period, for instance, and play a lot of music from this period. Then choose a specific composer, such as Bach, playing his different compositions until your child has a good idea of what Bach's music sounds like. After that you repeat one composition until your baby recognises that. This way, not only is the brain stimulated, but the child also gets to know the value of music and will later be able to identify different composers and their music.

Through the repetition of certain types of music, your baby becomes familiar with melody and rhythm. Nursery songs also have a role to play, as they are structured and repetitive by nature.

Here are some examples of composers and their music to get you on track:

- **J.S. BACH** (baroque period)
  Air on the G String; Concerto for Two Violins in D minor; Orchestral Suite No 2 in B minor and No 3 in D; Toccata and Fugue in D minor for Organ
- **BEETHOVEN** (classical period)
  Overtures; Moonlight Sonatas; Symphony No 5 in C minor and No 8 in F
- **BERLIOZ** (romantic period)
  Symphony Fantastique
- **CHOPIN** (late romantic period)
  Piano Concerto No 1 in E minor
- **HÄNDEL** (baroque period)
  Water Music Suite; Messiah; Music for the Royal Fireworks
- **HAYDN** (classical period)
  String Quartet No 77 in C; Symphony No 88 in G
- **MENDELSSOHN** (early romantic period)
  Symphony No 4 in A; Violin Concerto in E minor
- **SCHUBERT** (early romantic period)
  Symphony No 8 in B minor
- **SCHUMANN** (early romantic period)
  Symphony No 1 in B flat; 'Lieder'
- **VIVALDI**
  The Four Seasons

Music can be combined with a variety of other activities, making for lots of fun when making or listening to music with your baby. As with any other game an adult plays with a baby or child, you will have to free the child in you in order to make the best of the time spent with your child! Rhythm is the first musical aspect that a baby responds to, so clap your hands, stamp your feet and encourage your baby to move to the beat of the music. You can also use rattles (shakers), or even make your own with different sounds by filling different containers with buttons, seeds and beads. The visual effect of transparent containers could keep a baby entertained for some time!

---

1. Frances H. Rauscher, 'Can Music Instruction Affect Children's Cognitive Development?', in: *ERIC Digest* (ERIC identifier: ED480540, source: ERIC Clearinghouse on Early Education and Parenting, University of Illinois, September 2003).

6

Motor development

Motor skills are tasks involving the skeleton muscles of the body, in other words the movement of the various limbs and body parts. This includes eye-muscle movement, which enables a young baby to follow people in his close proximity with his eyes and assists older children with tasks such as reading and catching a ball.

While speech development is dependent on the efficient development of the speech organs and the muscles responsible for the movement of the tongue, lips and speech organs, motor development depends on the development and integration of all the different senses. This makes sense: A child will not be able to walk properly if the information that the motor area of his brain receives from his foot soles is incorrect or incorrectly interpreted. Neither will he be able to walk if the impulses from the inner ear, where balance is registered, are faulty. All the games used for the stimulation of sensory integration will also stimulate motor development. In figure 5 (see page 50) the integration of senses is right at the bottom, taking place first and followed by the development of motor aspects such as body image, motor planning, balance and lateralisation.

Motor development always follows a pattern inherent in the human species. Although the *tempo* at which it takes place may differ from child to child (and still be within 'normal' limits), the *order* is always the same. The baby develops from his head to his feet, i.e. downward, and from his body midline to his sides, i.e. outward. Downward development implies that the baby gains motor control of his neck and head before gaining control of his torso and hips, while outward development implies that he gains control of his torso and shoulders or hips before he can control his hands and fingers, or feet and toes.

The development is such that the child's initial reactions are general, i.e. involving the whole body. As he grows and develops, the reactions become more specific. For example, when a young baby hears a loud sound, his whole body jerks, whereas an older child will look in the direction of the sound, moving only his head and neck.

Development happens *continually* and *uninterruptedly*, and although the child goes from one stage to the next without pauses or interruptions, his individual development tempo is determined by heredity and environment. Each system and organ in the body also develops at its own tempo. For example, 80 per cent of the brain mass is fully developed by the age of two, while the sex organs remain fairly undeveloped until puberty, whereafter rapid development takes place.

It is interesting to note the normal pattern of motor development in your child as he grows older. Remember that as the development tempo for each person differs, any references to age in this book are merely guidelines. The successive development of motor skills does, however, allow the parent to know what can be expected from the baby after he has mastered a certain task. For example, he will not be able to sit on his own before he has first learned to roll over.

Head control. At the age of four weeks, eye movements and eye control are so well developed that the baby can follow a person around the room with his eyes. By about three months he can smile back at someone who smiles at him and by four months, he has fairly good eye coordination, enabling him to follow various objects, including moving people and a moving toy, with his eyes.

From the age of one month he can lift his head, holding it up for a few seconds when lying in the stomach position, and by four months, he has good head and neck control when held in the sitting position.

Torso control. By two months, the baby can turn from the side position to the back position, and by four months from his back to his side. Keep a watchful eye when he lies on a bed now, as he can instantly slip off!

Although torso control is seldom so well developed that a baby can sit without support before the age of six months, by four months the parent can start pulling him up into the sitting position. By five months he can sit with support, and by nine months he should be sitting strongly without any assistance.

Stool control normally begins at around two years of age, while bladder control can take anything from two to four years.

Arms and hands. Protective movements of the arms and hands can be noticed from the age of two weeks, albeit very general movements. By four months, the movements become more specific, with the baby reaching out to seize an object. Although by five months he can seize and hold an object, letting go only follows later (as many a mother who has tried to free an earring or strand of hair from her baby's grip can testify!). Using the fingers to pick up a small object, with the thumb in the up position (i.e. in a different direction with regard to the other fingers), is a pretty complex task that babies only master around eight months of age.

Legs and feet. Before a baby can crawl, he can stand in the crawling position, sometimes becoming very agitated not knowing how to move forward! Crawling movements (lying in the stomach position while pulling himself forward with his arms and kicking with his legs) help to get rid of some of the frustration. The baby first crawls on his hands and knees, before advancing to his hands and feet.

The baby gradually starts to pull himself up against furniture, standing with support until he can later stand alone. Then he starts to walk, first with assistance and later without.

Acquiring motor skills

Although motor development is dependent on genes and the pattern of human development, the more complex, and in particular the 'social' motor abilities, do not develop through maturing alone – they have to be acquired. These are normally skills that ensure socially acceptable behaviour, as well as those inherent to a specific culture.

There are some specific factors that positively influence the acquirement of motor abilities. For example, when a child receives little or no guidance when he starts to eat with a spoon, this ability is acquired more slowly and less efficiently than when the child is shown how to use a spoon. The unguided child will probably not know how to use the spoon in a socially acceptable manner either. In another culture, the child may learn to use different eating utensils, or even none at all. Some people reckon that when a skill is acquired in an improper way, it takes 35 repetitions to get out of the wrong habit and into the right one. If this is true, it makes a lot of sense to help a child learn a skill correctly from the outset.

The following factors are imperative for the acquirement of motor skills:

- The child must be ripe for learning the skill, having reached the required stage of development.
- Learning opportunities must be created if they do not exist naturally in the environment.
- Opportunities must be created for practising newly acquired skills.
- A good example and role model are important – children learn a great deal from what they see others do.
- Efficient guidance and support, aimed at helping the child to make a success, will encourage him to approach a task with confidence.
- Both children and adults need motivation in order to learn.

- Each motor skill should be learned individually, preferably one at a time. You cannot teach your child how to eat with a spoon, a knife and a fork all in one day. First teach him how to use a spoon efficiently before advancing to the more complex tasks.

There are specific methods of learning motor skills that are used by babies, children and adults alike. Whether it is a baby learning to eat with a spoon, or an athlete learning to do the high jump, one of the following methods will be used:

1. With the **trial-and-error method** there is no guidance and no model to follow, and the acquired skill is usually not performed to the person's best potential.
2. **Imitation** is the learning of a skill by watching and copying a model. Although faster than trial-and-error, this method is subject to the mistakes that the model makes.
3. Proper **coaching** takes place when the learning is guided and supervised. The model demonstrates the skill and makes sure that the task is executed correctly. This is especially important during the early stages of learning, preventing the improper acquiring of skills and methods.

The importance of motor skills

Motor skills are not only necessary for tasks such as learning to walk or learning to play a sport later on, but also essential in teaching a child to operate independently and functionally in his daily life. The following are the functional categories of skills that a child has to acquire:

- **Self-sufficiency.** The child needs to learn skills that will help him become independent. These include eating, dressing himself, combing his hair, washing his face, brushing his teeth and washing his body.
- **Social skills.** To be accepted as a group member, the child must make a meaningful contribution to that group, be it family, school or society. Skills that enable the child to help the group with its tasks, lead to acceptance by the group.
- **Play skills.** To be able to play in the group and to entertain himself when he is alone, the child has to acquire skills such as ball play, cycling, drawing, painting and the manipulation of toys.
- **School skills.** Much of the work done at school (and preschool) is based on motor skills – including writing, drawing, painting, clay play and dancing. The better these skills are developed, the easier the child will adjust to the school and to the non-academic activities at the school.

Stimulating motor development

The different aspects of motor development can be stimulated with games, examples of which are given below:

Balance

Balance is the ability to maintain a certain body position, of which sitting is the first. As balance is controlled by the vestibular system, games that will stimulate this system (see chapter 5) can also be used for stimulating balance. Good balance entails the maintenance of positions and postures against gravity, providing a firm basis for the performance of other tasks. *Static balance* is balance without movement (e.g. standing on one leg), while *dynamic balance* refers to balance during movement (e.g. walking on a balance beam).

IMPROVING BALANCE IN BABIES WHO HAVE NOT YET LEARNED TO SIT
During this stage, it is especially important to stimulate the vestibular system and the torso muscles, teaching the baby to maintain the sitting position. This includes the games described in the chapter on sensory development. Also encourage your baby to roll over to both sides, from the stomach as well as the back position. Laying him down in the stomach position encourages him to lift up his head in order to look at objects in the environment, strengthening his back muscles as well as the extensors at the back of his neck. Laying your baby down in the back position and pulling him up by his hands while he lifts up his head, will strengthen his stomach muscles as well as the flexors at the front of his neck. Strengthening these muscle groups is important for maintaining balance in the sitting position.

IMPROVING BALANCE IN BABIES WHO CAN SIT BY THEMSELVES, BUT HAVE NOT
   YET LEARNED TO CRAWL
When a baby first learns to sit, it is in a position with a wide base of support. He not only uses his buttocks as support, but also places his hands in front of his legs, carrying weight on his hands as well in order to widen the base of support and more easily maintain his balance. As the baby gets older, he will be able to lift his hands off the floor, carrying weight on his buttocks only. Initially he is fairly unsteady, but soon he sits comfortably, his hands free to perform other tasks such as picking up toys and bringing them to his mouth, extending his arms to be picked up, and stretching them out to get hold of an object. At this stage, the baby can also be encouraged to stand on all fours, getting ready to crawl.

   Babies who do not like lying in the stomach position are often not keen to stand on all fours either, and will sometimes shuffle along on their buttocks rather than crawl. The crawling action teaches a baby to use opposite arm and leg movements, necessary for lateralisation (identifying left and right) and laying the foundation for rhythmic movements, which is the reason why it is desirable for every baby to crawl for a few months of his life.

If your baby refuses to crawl, however, you can regularly play the games for vestibular stimulation, especially those that require lying in the stomach position and lifting up the head, strengthening the back neck muscles.

You can also do the following:

- Sit on the carpet with your legs stretched in front of you, laying your baby over your thigh in the crawling position. Put objects on the floor, encouraging him to pick them up and give them to you, making sure that he regularly lifts up and holds his head high. Also make sure that your baby carries weight on his hands and/or knees, strengthening his shoulder and/or hip muscles.
- Lay your baby in the stomach position over a ball (larger than a soccer ball) or a small rolled-up mattress. Now roll the ball until your baby's hands press on the floor and carry weight. Then roll the ball to the opposite side, his feet pressing on the floor and carrying weight. Make it a slow rocking movement between your baby's hands and feet. The baby normally starts to enjoy this after a while.
- To encourage your baby to move, lay him down in the stomach position on the floor or carpet, placing toys just outside his reach. Trying to seize them will encourage him to stretch, and hopefully also push with his knee.

Do not force your baby to crawl before he is ready. Only once he starts to use other ways of moving forward, such as dragging himself along on his buttocks, is this an indication that he is ready to move from one place to another, and crawling may be encouraged. Before he is motivated to move forward, both you and your baby will find it easier, and more enjoyable, to play the games for sensory stimulation and improving balance in the sitting position, rather than trying to force something that he is not ready for yet.

IMPROVING BALANCE IN BABIES WHO CAN CRAWL, BUT HAVE NOT YET LEARNED TO WALK

At this stage, a baby usually needs little motivation to practise his newly acquired skills. He enjoys the movement and his freedom to move from one point to the next – even among a number of points in the house. The baby now keeps his parents quite busy, as he needs to be watched constantly and often needs to be run after. He explores the world and moves independently in familiar environments such as his house, while in unfamiliar environments, he usually only moves inside the parent's field of vision, regularly returning to the parent.

As the baby crawls and moves, he strengthens all the muscles needed for pulling himself up and standing on his feet, and eventually starting to walk. The period from the baby's first unsteady crawling movements until he starts to walk is seldom longer than three months. Ample crawling opportunity usually provides good exercise for strengthening of the major muscle groups and stimulation of the vestibular system, in order to maintain balance in the standing position.

IMPROVING BALANCE IN BABIES WHO HAVE STARTED TO WALK

As a baby's first steps are usually fairly unsteady, he often reverts to crawling when wanting to move fast. This is completely acceptable and normal. Encourage your baby to walk by letting him walk from one parent to the other, or from something that he is holding onto to a parent. Most parents play this game spontaneously, as they love watching the miracle of their child taking his first steps and enjoy sharing in his new skill. Start by holding his hand until his leg, hip and torso muscles have been given enough exercise to remain in the upright position when he moves. Initially he will only be able to walk barefoot on a level floor, as bare feet offer more resistance than slippery soles on a slippery floor. However, he will soon master different floor surfaces as well as different shoe types. Holding his hand when walking on unfamiliar surfaces will help him feel comfortable and secure.

Good balance is imperative if a child is to enjoy movements such as walking and running, also providing a good basis for participation in any sport or activity, like dancing. The following games are aimed at improving balance:

1. The parent crouches on all fours while the child lies on the parent's back, holding on tightly. Pretending to be a wild horse, the parent moves up and down, slowly at first to test the child's ability, and then increasing the degree of 'wildness'. The child holds on, trying to remain on the back of this wild horse trying to throw him. Of course this will only work if the child is fairly small and the parent strong enough! Be careful not to get hurt, watching your back in particular. This game exercises the child's shoulder and arm flexors, and sometimes also the leg and stomach muscles.
2. The child crouches on all fours (for added fun the parent can assume the same position) while a ball is being rolled towards him. Bending his elbows, he then rolls the ball back with his head. In another interesting version, the ball can be rolled towards a target. This game exercises equilibrium reactions for improved balance.
3. Both the child and the parent stand on their knees, using a ball to play 'knee soccer'. Only the knees are employed for rolling the ball, attempting to score a 'goal' (improvise with a cardboard box or a chair). Serving to improve equilibrium reactions and balance, this game can be great fun when the whole family plays along.
4. The child stands with his legs apart while the parent rolls a ball between his legs from behind. The child catches the ball, throwing it back to the parent over his head.
5. The child walks along a sticky-tape or chalk line on the floor, trying not to step off the line at all. A younger child can try to stay between two lines, while from about four years of age, a single line can be used. The next step would be to walk on a balance beam or a plank lying on the floor.

Bilateral integration and lateralisation

Bilateral integration and lateralisation involve the collaboration between the two sides (left and right) of the body, in other words the two hands or two feet. Efficient bilateral integration later on enables a child to eat with a knife and fork, use scissors with ease and write with one hand while holding the book or paper with the other. The first practical signs that bilateral integration is starting to develop are when the baby can hold his bottle by himself and when he can hold two objects, one in each hand. He then begins to hit the two objects together and also to clap his hands. As this skill improves, the baby will start to pass an object from one hand to the other. Later on he will be able to use his two hands for different tasks, such as holding a bowl with one hand and handling a spoon with the other.

Lateralisation goes hand in hand with bilateral integration, developing the concept of left and right, and later also of position and spatial orientation, helping the child with concepts such as above and below, inside and outside, and letters like 'b' and 'd' (the same shape, but one facing right and the other left). Proper development of this aspect results in better reading and spelling abilities.

As the crawling action provides excellent exercise for bilateral integration and lateralisation, your baby should not be encouraged to start walking too soon. The longer he crawls, the more these important aspects will be stimulated. The following games can also be used for stimulating bilateral integration and lateralisation in a baby who has already started to walk:

1. The child sits on the floor, leaning backwards with his weight on his hands, and his feet in the air. The parent then rolls a ball towards the child's feet, encouraging him to kick it back to the parent. This game exercises shoulder stability and the torso flexors, as well as simultaneous movements of the feet.
2. The child lies in the stomach position on a small blanket on a slippery floor, with toys such as shapes or jigsaw puzzle pieces packed out around him. Using his arms to spin himself around, he picks up one shape or piece at a time, turning back with his head lifted up, aiming to complete the shape-sorter or puzzle. This game exercises the neck and back extensors as well as successive arm movements.
3. Lying in the stomach position on smooth cardboard or a small blanket placed on a slippery floor, with his arms stretched out and his legs lifted up, the child pretends to be an aeroplane. Using both legs, he kicks against a wall, trying to 'fly' as far as possible. This game, which can also be played by two or more children, strengthens the neck, shoulder and back extensors, while also exercising simultaneous leg movements.
4. The child sits on the floor (an older child can stand on one or both legs), while the parent rolls the ball slightly to the left or right of the child, encouraging him to stop, catch and roll it back. The ball must be large enough to be handled with both hands, in order to encourage the child to make the necessary handling

adjustments. This game is aimed at exercising equilibrium reactions (which are necessary for balance), as well as bilateral movements, and encouraging lateralisation.
5. Let your child play with shaving cream in the bath, encouraging him to use both hands simultaneously to make patterns on the wall tiles. Most children enjoy the sensation of touching the foam, while using both hands stimulates bilateral integration and lateralisation. Finger paint can also be used for painting on large sheets of newsprint. Taping the newsprint to a low window or tiles will minimise cleaning up afterwards.
6. Using balls of different sizes, textures and weights, play any ball game that encourages your baby to roll and catch the ball. Later on the child can be encouraged to throw the ball instead of rolling it.
7. Tearing paper stimulates bilateral movement. Your baby will enjoy this activity, and even more so when he sees the approval on your face! This 'destructive' task can be converted into something positive by using the torn paper for making papier-mâché (see recipes in appendix 2, page 157).
8. Stringing beads can be great fun from the age of about two years, beginning with large beads and relatively thick, strong string.

Motor planning

Motor planning is the planning that precedes a motor action. Although this happens in split seconds and on an unconscious level, without motor planning a child will be clumsy, dropping and breaking objects, falling often and approaching tasks clumsily and awkwardly. Adults with poor motor-planning skills are clumsy, struggle to follow instructions and easily lose their way.

Although motor planning can hardly be stimulated with any specific games, stimulation does happen during participation in various activities. If the child is clumsy or performs poorly in motor activities, the parent should divide the task into simpler units, using one of the three methods on page 72 to help the child acquire the skill. The child then repeats the task until it is performed efficiently. The different steps for the successful performance of a task are taught cognitively, allowing the child to learn and perform the task step by step. The more tasks a child learns to do in this manner, the easier he will later find it to divide a task by himself, approaching it step by step. In the young toddler this applies to tasks such as dressing himself, while in the older child it can be something like organising his schoolwork, tidying his room or reorganising his cupboard.

Poor motor-planning skills make efficient functioning impossible, so if your child has a problem in this regard, he should be assisted with learning the necessary tasks as early as possible. For example, if you discover that your child finds it difficult to fit shapes into a shape-sorter, you can first try the trial-and-error method. If he still does not succeed, you can teach him to (1) look at the shape, (2) find its place on the shape-sorter, (3) turn the shape into the correct position and (4) insert the shape.

Children who have a problem with motor planning are often very impatient, as they probably struggle with more tasks than what we are aware of and want to finish a task as quickly as possible in order to 'get away' from it. These children often shy away from participating in activities such as building jigsaw puzzles, sorting shapes and even colouring in or cutting and pasting, rather choosing to go outside where they can swing or play in the sand. This way they can avoid tasks that require planning, escaping to tasks where nobody can see them struggle and where there are no specific 'rules' to adhere to.

If a child tries to 'escape' in this manner, the last thing you should do is to compare him with others or to expect him to perform a task without assistance, or even make fun of him for running away. The child, knowing that he struggles long before a parent even notices it, tries his best to hide his inability. Take him by the hand, assuring him of your assistance and give him the reassurance that you will not do a task on his behalf, because you know that he can do it himself. What you *will* do, is to explain the different steps that will make the task easier for him, and be there should he need any help.

The task is then explained and performed step by step, with the parent offering support throughout. This way the child's trust in the parent and his confidence and his self-image remain intact, while the parent experiences less frustration and less impatience. By learning to divide a task and doing it step by step, the child also gains the confidence to approach future tasks on his own, instead of bluntly refusing to participate in an unfamiliar task.

Motor development is built upon successful sensory development, forming the basis for the development of higher cognitive tasks such as visual and auditory perception, and memory and concentration, which are necessary for efficient adaptation.

Gross motor movements

Gross motor movements are the big body movements which include movements of the torso, arms and legs. As explained earlier in the chapter, this starts with head control. Gross motor development can be stimulated by encouraging any movements. Remember that development follows a specific pattern, and that a baby will need to have good head control, in other words, a strong neck, before he can roll over. Similarly good torso control (in other words strong stomach and back muscles that make rolling movements possible), will be needed before the baby can sit or start crawling.

Movement is stimulated by motivation. Although a child will eventually learn to move without any motivation to do so, movement should be stimulated by encouraging the child to move. Movement is inhibited when a baby remains buckled up in his comfortable stroller or baby seat for hours. There are often toys in front of him which he can look at and reach for, keeping him happy and releasing his parents from having to watch him all the time. Although this may stimulate visual development (provided that the toys are alternated regularly) and teach your baby to seize and let go of objects, no gross motor movements are stimulated.

To stimulate gross motor movements, the baby has to be removed from the stroller or chair. His neck muscles will not be strengthened when his head is supported by the back rest for long periods of time; neither will his torso control be stimulated if he is not given the opportunity to roll over and try to sit by himself. Vestibular stimulation (the experience of movement) is also inhibited, being limited to the restricted movements in the stroller – a one-way movement whereby no input-output learning is allowed.

When the baby is encouraged to move, the large muscles are motivated to move. Placing toys just outside his reach encourages your baby to move or to reach for them. (Do not frustrate your baby by doing this too often, however!) A young baby will follow a person around the room with his eyes. Moving further away from the baby encourages head movements, as he is forced to turn his head in order to follow the person. Always putting objects in your baby's hands might keep him happy, but will not encourage him to reach for, or to move in, the direction of the objects himself. Similarly, a crawling baby is encouraged to pull himself up against furniture when he wants to investigate or get hold of an object lying on top. Encouraging gross motor movements further teaches the baby frustration endurance, as well as the concept of cause and effect.

Fine motor movements

Fine motor movements are the movements of the hands and fingers. Without strong torso and shoulder muscles these movements will not be possible. For example, in order to use a pencil efficiently the child must be able to sit upright, stabilise his shoulder and perform accurate eye movements. The various hand grasps develop according to a pattern, which is the same in all children. Initially a baby only reaches for an object. Through the reaction that takes place when he touches the object, the baby learns that his action causes a reaction. Later on he learns to seize and hold the object, and still later to let go of the object. The hand grasps are as follows:

- *Ulnar grasp:* An object, such as an adult's finger, is held in the palm of the baby's hand, being grasped with the index, middle, ring and little fingers. Involving no thumb action, this is also the grasp used by chimpanzees. When an object is placed in the hand of a newborn baby, the grasp happens reflexively, while later on it is also used voluntarily when the baby holds a rattle or toy being placed in his hand.
- *Palmar grasp:* All five fingers of the hand are involved in holding an object. Hold your hand above a golf ball lying on a table, then pick it up with all five fingers, touching the ball at the same time. This is the grasp that young babies use for picking up and holding specific objects. As the thumb is now also involved, this grasp differentiates your baby from the higher animal species such as the chimpanzee.
- *Lateral grasp:* The baby now uses his thumb and most of the remaining four fingers for picking up objects. He can, for example, pull a peg from a peg board or hold a wooden jigsaw puzzle piece by its knob.

- The baby then starts to use his index finger, pushing it into the holes of a peg board, for instance. This is also the stage at which wall sockets become very inviting, so do make sure that your house is safe to prevent your baby from hurting himself.
- The baby now manages to pick up objects and put them down, enabling him to throw blocks into a container, for example. Most babies enjoy packing them in, only to throw everything out again. Do not be concerned – he is exercising the hand and finger movements that will enable him to grasp a pencil soon.
- *Pinching grasp:* The baby uses his thumb and index finger to pick up small objects. As this is a new challenge, your baby will notice all sorts of small objects, so be especially careful not to leave pills, buttons and small beads lying around the house – he may still want to investigate objects with his mouth, posing the danger of poisoning or choking.
- By approximately one year of age, the baby begins to scribble, using the palmar grasp for holding the pencil. Although this may look clumsy, it is an important step in his development. Chubby crayons, suitable for little hands, are readily available, while chubby chalk, better known as pavement chalk, is also convenient at this stage of development. Vertical lines are scribbled before horizontal lines, with diagonal lines and circles only following later.
- The baby can now insert, as well as let go of, pegs in a peg board. He can also turn the pages of a cardboard book by himself, later advancing to the pages of an ordinary book without assistance. The action of letting go enables the baby to build a tower with blocks – as vertical lines precede horizontal lines, he will master a 'tower' before building a 'train'.
- By this time the baby can spoon-feed himself and use a drinking cup quite efficiently.

By practising the various fine motor tasks the baby becomes more dextrous, his grasp developing into the three-finger pencil grasp that he will start using around the age of five years. Although babies and toddlers play with relatively large objects, as they develop, smaller and finer finger movements can be expected, until they are able to thread small beads onto thin string and write with a pen. Always keep in mind that a child needs good balance, posture and shoulder control for the efficient performance of fine finger movements, which is why the practising of balance, gross motor movements, bilateral movements and motor planning should remain a priority.

7
Body image

A child whose sensory systems and motor skills develop optimally, will possess a healthy body image, involving a good perception of his own body, the various body parts, their sizes, functions, abilities and names, as well as of his body in relation to the environment outside his body. He begins to see himself as an individual in an environment that poses certain demands and expectations on him, some of which he can meet and others he cannot. This way he gets to know himself, as well as his abilities, better.

Body image development starts early in the young baby and is a continual process. Our bodies changing throughout our lives – we grow, we become bigger and stronger, thinner or fatter, less or more muscular, and when we are older, our hair colour changes and our skins become wrinkly! Our body image must adapt to these changes continually. Someone who suddenly loses or gains weight often finds it difficult to know instinctively which clothes will fit him or her, while someone who has maintained the same body weight for years often knows immediately, by merely looking at a garment, whether it is the right size and cut. A young baby is yet to learn where his different body parts fit in, what they are called, and what they are used for.

Body image develops when a baby's brain receives sensory messages from the limbs and various organs, including the skin. Young babies often play with their fingers or feet by touching or sucking them, resulting in various messages being sent to the brain, where they are processed and stabilised to create a body image, among other things. A child who has just started to crawl, will bump his head a few times while attempting to pass under a coffee table, not realising how low it is, or how big his head is. However, very soon he does it without bumping his head, which goes to show how fast and efficiently he learns and adapts, thanks to all the sensory messages reaching his brain.

When a baby or child participates in motor activities and games, he also learns about the size of his body and the abilities of his various body parts. Through sensory impulses from the organs such as the stomach and lungs (e.g. stomach cramps or hunger pangs and the fast, deep breathing even a young child experiences after exercise), he learns about the functions of the organs. Even babies get out of breath after crawling some distance!

So we see that the development of a healthy body image depends on the sensory impulses received by the brain during activities that stimulate the various senses, as well as motor development. A child who regularly participates in a variety of these activities, should naturally develop a healthy body image.

The cognitive aspects of body image, i.e. the names and functions of the child's different body parts, and the ability of each in comparison to the other body parts (as well as other children and adults), should, however, be taught by the parent. This can easily happen during the normal daily routine by regularly mentioning the names of body parts, as well as their functions, where applicable. By calling out the names of the limbs as you wash your baby, for example, he will soon get to know them, together with his first words. The same goes for organs and their functions: Before the child is fed, for instance, you articulate his feelings by saying something like, "Are you hungry? Is your stomach empty?" and after he has been fed, you say, "Do you feel better now? Is your stomach full?" This often comes naturally, as this is how most parents talk to their babies and children anyway.

This can only happen, however, if the child is taken care of by a parent or another competent person. If he is left in the care of a person who speaks another language, or hardly speaks at all, or someone who fails to heed these simple principles, it could lead to lags at a later stage.

The informed parent, or trained carer, will also naturally follow up on this conversation as the child gets older, saying something like, "You were hungry, but when you eat, your stomach gets full. The food is digested and taken through your blood stream to many parts of your body, enabling you to grow and play. When you eat too much and your stomach becomes too full, the digested food turns into fat. This is unhealthy and can make us sick. That is why we should not eat too much." In this way the basic concepts of health and good eating habits are instilled, even though the child is too young to talk himself. Of course you will not give a two-year-old all the information at once, but if the aspects are repeated regularly, you will be surprised by the young age at which your child will be grasping and repeating the concepts. By doing this, you help the child enlarge his vocabulary, expand his understanding and image of his own body, and teach him his first lessons in healthy eating habits – all of these within a few minutes, with no preparation or extra tasks and games required!

A well-developed body image provides the child with the knowledge necessary for grasping the concept of left and right. Because this is so important for reading and writing, it is heavily emphasised by educators in the year before the child goes to school. However, the concept of left and right is built on a healthy body image, leading to a good sense of spatial positioning and spatial relativity. Spatial conception – above and below, up and down, back and front, inside and outside, next to, long and short, fat and thin, big and small, and later also diagonally left and right – develops when the child starts to perceive objects around him in relation to his body and to one another. This happens when, during participation in gross and fine motor activities, impulses are sent from the various limbs, the skin and other senses (such as the eyes), to the different brain areas, where the synapses are stabilised through repetition.

There is no need, however, to wait until the year before your child goes to school to start teaching him about spatial positioning and spatial relativity through cognitive tasks. These can be stimulated from a very young age, so that by the time the child goes to school and is expected to do formal schoolwork, he will already have a good grasp of the concepts.

It may well happen that a child has a lag of unknown origin and that, even though he was well stimulated as a baby and young toddler, he can still experience problems with these concepts when confronted with them in two-dimensional school tasks. If that is the case, professional advice should be sought – the sooner the better. A proper evaluation will point out the problem areas, enabling the therapist to prescribe exercises which could be done either during therapy or at home. Dyslexic children often have difficulty with grasping these particular concepts, among others. The causes having been debated for decades, experts have come up with various (sometimes contradictory) reasons. Nevertheless, efficient stimulation during the baby and toddler years will diminish if not completely prevent problems.

Body image development takes place following various successive steps as the child gets older. These steps can be summarised as follows:

1. **Knowledge of the body parts.** The child gets to know the names of the various body parts. The easiest way of teaching this is to regularly say the names while dressing or bathing the child or when playing games. Also point out your own and other people's, body parts to the child. The names of body parts are often some of the first words that a child recognises. He can usually point to different body parts *on himself* before he can name them, or point them out *on other people*.
2. **Two-dimensional images.** Once the child knows his own body parts, he can start pointing them out on other people, toys and later also in books. Even when he can

already point out the more obvious parts such as 'eyes' in books, he may still be unsure of other, less obvious parts, such as 'throat', on himself.

3. **Location.** After further development the child will be able to complete a simple jigsaw puzzle of the human body, or if he cannot build the puzzle himself, he will be able to show you where the pieces should go. For example, when you ask him what part it is that he is holding (e.g. 'hand'), he will be able to point to his own hand and show you where to insert the piece before he can even say the word. However, as children vary greatly, there could be many variations with regard to their development.

4. **Reproduction.** The older child will try to draw a human figure, his first attempt usually being only a circle for the head, maybe accompanied by two dots for the eyes and a line for the mouth or sometimes for the legs or arms. Due to the variation in children's exposure and experiences, development of this skill varies from child to child.

If a child finds it difficult to remember and point out the different body parts, playful repetition of the names as in step 1 overleaf is the best answer. Drilling or trying to employ cognitive abilities will be of little use.

If the child struggles to locate body parts or makes no attempt at drawing them, continue playing games as in step 1, but also try the following:

- Using face paint or coloured soap, paint the child's body parts in different colours, naming the parts. Then have the child lie down on a large sheet of paper or cardboard and trace his outline. Paint the body parts on the paper the same colours as on his body. Let him look at the resemblance in a mirror, once again naming the parts.
- Using different textures, for instance a facecloth, silk scarf, soft brush (e.g. the mushroom brush sold in supermarkets) and cellulite brush, and different temperatures such as a water bottle from the refrigerator and a microwave-heated wheat bag, brush or stroke the child's different body parts. Name the body parts as you stroke on the left and right, back and front. Do this daily before or after bath time. Repeat the names while undressing, washing and dressing your child.
- Again have the child lie down on a large sheet of paper or cardboard, tracing his outline as you name the body parts. He then gets up and repeats the names, with the parent's help if necessary. Cut the different body parts out of the paper. (Be sure to ask the child's permission first, assuring him that the pieces will be glued together again – some children get quite upset when 'they' are being cut up!) Stick the body parts to a wall, following the child's instructions as to where they should go. If there is a large mirror in the room, the child will be able to see that his neck is below his head, for example, followed by his torso, with his arms on either side of the torso, the legs at the bottom and his hands and feet in their places.

- Using songs like 'Simple Simon' and the many others available on tape or CD, enjoy the music with your child, repeating it over and over again.
- Looking through old magazines with your child, encourage him to find a body part that he already knows, such as 'eyes'. Let him point out the eyes on all pictures of humans and animals. The parent then chooses a body part unfamiliar to the child, such as 'hip', pointing it out to him in each picture. Then it is the child's turn again to point at something that he knows. This way the child gets to experience joy and success as he learns.
- Use large objects such as cardboard boxes to build with. Young children also enjoy using furniture and blankets to build dens inside the house. Apart from being excellent fantasy play, this is great for teaching the child about positioning, spatial concepts and his body in relation to other objects. If you have enough space, a few cardboard boxes in a garage are ideal for building houses, cages for toy animals or hiding places – providing some of the best stimulation for spatial concepts and body image that a child can get. The young child will need assistance and build simpler structures. Although the ability to build something like a cage or pen only develops by around four or five years of age, and a two-year-old will probably only build 'trains' or 'towers', the parent can play with him, guiding him and giving him excellent stimulation.

In my therapy sessions, I often see primary school children with a poor body image draw human figures far below the expectation for their age. Making use of textures and touch stimulation during therapy, even for children in this age group, results in huge improvements in their body image, as well as in their drawings of human figures within just a few short weeks. Stimulating your child at this 'simple' level is no waste of time! By addressing the root of the problem, excellent results are achieved.

Once your child has developed a good body image, knows most of the body parts and starts to draw or paint human figures, the concept of left and right can also be taught at a cognitive level by saying, 'left' and 'right' and telling him which hand he is using when picking up an object or using a pencil. However, only by the age of four or five years, will this concept be completely established.

8

Self-image

The word *self-image* is very descriptive, suggesting the image that a person has of himself or herself. It is a fact that emotional, and even health, conditions have an effect on a person's self-image. This is greatly influenced by the reaction of the people around you, 'reflecting images' back to you, almost like mirrors. Through these images, you get an idea of how other people feel about you, affecting the image that you have about yourself.

A child thinks of himself what the people in his immediate environment think of him, or rather, what they make him *believe* that they think of him. All people sometimes think more and other times less of themselves, depending on what is happening around them, in other words, the 'input' that they get from their environment. Although an adult can do much to improve his self-image (get fit, take part in an activity which brings him success, talk to someone who affirms him), we have all experienced how quickly this positive image can convert into a negative image through a single comment or remark by someone who may not even be aware of what he has done!

In order to achieve success and even begin to utilise one's potential, a positive self-image is indispensable. A good self-image implies that you like the person that you are, and that you accept yourself with all your abilities and limitations. You feel good, comfortable and relaxed about yourself. You do not spend too much time worrying or brooding over your weaknesses, shortcomings and imperfections. You are realistic about your flaws and inabilities, but you are just as realistic about the things that are good and positive about you.

It is important to help your children establish a positive self-image. This process starts at birth and continues throughout a person's life. It is, however, similarly important for parents and carers to possess a healthy self-image. Too often we see parents and carers who feel inferior, or who think that they are not educated enough and that other people know more than them. These feelings are conveyed to their children at a very young age. It is not uncommon to come across parents who are really ashamed of themselves and their children – when parents disregard their own value, they include their children in this view, disregarding their children's value as well. Therapists often hear remarks such as, "Our children are not so clever," "Our children will never be so well mannered" or "Our children are always the naughtiest." Unfortunately the children hear this, giving rise to a low opinion of themselves. This can, however, be prevented by encouraging a healthy self-image in the child from a very young age. A child believes what his parents tell him, and what he gathers from their body language, making them important role players in fostering a positive self-image and self-esteem in their child.

The first emotions that a baby experiences are emotional reactions to physical discomfort. The baby is hungry, he cries, he is fed and taken care of, he feels better and he is happy. This pattern is repeated until he learns that when he feels uncomfortable, he can cry and the discomfort will be removed. The baby is hereby convinced that he is important enough to evoke a response from his carers. As the people who constantly remove his discomfort become synonymous with the solution to his problem, he prefers to be taken care of by those who have already proven their affection and helped to make him feel good. Parents and carers who know the baby well, do not let him cry for a long time before taking care of him, but instead change his nappy and give him his bottle, as soon as he wakes up. His discomfort being replaced with love before he needs to start crying, he learns a positive way of attracting his carers' attention – as merely waking up and smiling attracts enough attention, there is no need for crying to make it happen! By showing love (smiling, cooing) he receives positive attention and love. This is his first lesson in giving and taking, in giving and receiving love. This child will possess a balanced love for himself as well as for other people.

On the other hand, a baby who regularly has an opposite experience, learns that he is not loved by others, that he cannot rely on his carers to make him happy and that he is unwanted. This baby will find it very hard to love himself and regard himself a worthy human being. Instead of giving and receiving love, he learns early on that he has to use negative methods to draw attention to his physical discomfort. His experiences lead to a contorted ability to love himself and other people, with the synapses, dendrites and nerve tracts formed and stabilised in his brain starting off on a false note as far as self-image and self-acceptance are concerned.

Happiness

So, it seems that babies and children who are well cared for, are happy children. Happiness plays an important role in every person's life, and no less in the life and development of a baby and child. A happy child is more adaptable than one who is unhappy. Affecting numerous aspects of a person's life, adaptability implies the difference between someone who can hold his own in a mature way and someone who depends on alternatives in order to deal with his day-to-day problems. These alternatives include various reactions, from a fast temper to alcohol or drug abuse.

The effect of happiness on a child's adaptability and handling of everyday problems can be summarised as follows:

- Happy children are healthy and full of energy, while unhappiness drains a child's power and energy, as well as his general physical wellbeing.
- Happy children convert their energy into purposeful activity, while the energy of unhappy children is wasted on daydreaming and self-pity.
- Happiness improves a child's physical appearance by putting a cheerful expression on his face, evoking positive reactions from others, while the expression of self-pity on the face of an unhappy child evokes negative reactions.
- Happiness inspires a child to do things, while an unhappy child is unmotivated.
- Happy children handle frustrations better, trying to understand the reasons behind them, while unhappy children react with anger, preventing them from understanding the reasons for their frustrations and learning how to solve these problems.
- Happiness encourages social contact, while unhappiness leads to reservedness and self-centredness.
- Happiness develops into a habit, and so does unhappiness.
- Although a happy childhood does not guarantee success as an adult, it does lay the foundation for success. Unhappiness lays the foundation for failure.

A happy child is a child whose needs are met and who gets what is required to keep him healthy and content. That does not imply, however, that spoiling a child with too many luxuries or an attitude of, 'Don't worry, Mommy will do or fix everything' can foster happiness. Balance and responsibility are indispensable qualities in parents and carers. (More about this in the chapters on parenthood and discipline.)

Happiness depends mainly on four aspects, which are also the four most important things that a child needs in his life:

1. **Acceptance.** A child feels accepted when he is loved, notwithstanding his shortcomings, peculiarities, lags or talents. Parents convey the message of acceptance by recognising the child's positive traits (e.g. a special talent, beautiful hair, a winsome

personality), as well as his negative traits (e.g. an inability to sing in tune, thin or fine hair, impatience) by mentioning them by name and confirming that they are part of his make-up, without using them to either sing his praises or run him down. In other words, the child is not judged by his positive and negative traits. By mentioning the traits by name, the child is guided to a better self-knowledge, while he also learns how to deal with the specific trait. (Positive traits also need to be handled correctly, as you do not want your child to look down on, or belittle, friends who do not possess the same positive characteristics.) In this way, the child is made aware of his traits without being judged by them. The trait may, however, be judged by making the child understand how proud you are of her beautiful hair or that his impatience makes you feel ashamed, the difference being that you do not make the child feel that her beautiful hair makes her better than anybody else or that his impatience makes him a bad person. The child gets to know himself and learns to accept that he has good and bad traits, just like everybody else has good and bad traits. This makes him feel that he is accepted just as he is, laying the foundation for the child to accept other people as they are.

2. **Love.** We already know that a baby experiences love when he is taken good physical care of. Similarly, older toddlers and children also need good physical care. Not only does the child see that people care for him, but he also learns that physical care is important, ensuring that, later on, he will take good care of his own body. As people generally react positively to someone who is physically attractive and well groomed, this is the beginning of numerous positive images that will be reflected back to your child throughout his life. A further affirmation of love is acceptance, as discussed above. Love also implies that parents spend ample time with their children. Saying that you love a child while often neglecting him, leaves the child with a feeling of abandonment – your actions contradicting your words. When the parent takes a lively interest in the child's life, interests and abilities, it makes him feel important and beloved. This interest in your child's world, which begins when playing with your baby and getting to know him, later expands to an interest in his school activities, his choice of friends and his preferences for games and tasks. Make an effort to become part of your child's world as well as to involve him in your world. Although going to work every day is inevitable, if your child sees from a young age where you are going to and which people you are working with, you will not just 'disappear' every morning – he will know where you are and be a part of your life. The same goes for your sports and hobbies.

3. **Success.** Every human being has the need to succeed, and also to be acknowledged for the successes that he achieves. Have you ever worked hard at a task, handed it in with pride and then felt devastated when you heard that it was not necessary to be done after all, and that it would be of no use to anyone? Remember that when your toddler comes to you with something that he has made, painted or even picked up.

Do not use praise unrealistically, but do keep in mind that whatever the child has made, has taken some special effort and deserves recognition from the parent. This also applies when he tells you a story or tries to sing you a new song. Do not compare his efforts with those of others. They can, however, be compared to his own previous efforts to see whether they have improved or in which ways they differ, giving him more insight in his own abilities, and making him feel that you are interested in what he does (by remembering what he did earlier). It should also inspire him to achieve success. Once again, this should be done without judging the child – only his effort is judged and compared with his own previous efforts. Positive comments also generate a feeling of success. Say, for example, "I like the green apple that you painted better than the red one," rather than, "The red apple is ugly."

4. **Moderate discipline.** Strict, steadfast rules have no place in a loving, supportive environment, and neither have harsh, pain-inflicting punitive measures. The child must know where he stands, what is right or wrong, and that wrong behaviour has negative and unpleasant consequences. Consistency is the key to discipline. What is regarded wrong today, must also be wrong tomorrow and the next day, and what is regarded right today, must also be right tomorrow and the next day. Explain rules to your baby from a very young age. When a baby tries to touch a hot stove plate, most parents say, "No! Ouch!", implying that if he touches it, he will get hurt. We sometimes forget to give this same guidance when the child gets older, or often, with a house full of children, our time is just so limited that we simply do not get around to giving explanations. It is okay if this happens occasionally – children must learn that we do not always have time and that sometimes they must simply obey. Parents must, however, make time to explain, and especially to make positive comments. Avoid saying *"No!"* too often, as this can be destructive. A baby or young child who does not receive positive attention, will seek negative attention, which could degenerate into a vicious circle. More about this in chapter 14.

A happy, well-adjusted child almost always develops a healthy self-image – the two go hand in hand.

Fostering a healthy self-image

The following are the most important aspects needed for the development of a healthy self-image:
- the feeling that you belong somewhere and that you are loved
- the feeling that you have value and significance
- the feeling that you are competent and have the abilities that are expected of you

Only three things to ensure a positive self-image in your child! However, this is sometimes easier said than done. Below are some practical examples that parents can use during a normal day, not only to build a precious relationship with their child, but also to ensure that the child builds a positive image of himself:

1. **Meeting physical needs.** A child cannot value himself if he is not taken good physical care of – so do pay attention to your child's diet, clothes and personal grooming. Spending time with a child by grooming him and making him feel attractive will enable him to approach his day with confidence. A well-groomed appearance ensures positive reactions from other people, helping to build the child's self-image. Note that I am not saying that a child should be dandified, but that he should be clean and tidy, well fed, looking healthy and happy.

    This also includes the child's body language. Because a child does not have the verbal ability that an adult has to articulate his feelings, desires and needs, a parent must be sensitive to the messages that a child expresses through his body language, acting appropriately and consistently. Body language speaks where vocabulary and language ability fall short, and parents who are mindful of their child's body language and facial expressions will be able to 'read' his feelings. Getting to know this aspect of your child enables you to act proactively when something is worrying him.

2. **Reassuring contact.** A child needs love and warmth. Touch your child, hug him, cuddle him, make eye contact – that is what he yearns for. It makes him feel lovable, loved and worthy of your love.

3. **Choices.** Show your child that you trust him by giving him choices. Even a very young child should be given choices, teaching him that his opinion counts and that he has control over parts of his life. Asking him, "Would you like milk or orange juice?", for instance, makes him feel that you think he is capable of making a choice. He also learns that when he has made a choice, he must bear the consequences.

4. **Positive comments.** Regularly comment on what your child has done right. This is often neglected, while we hardly hesitate to comment when the child has done something wrong. If you are proud of him, he will also be proud of himself. It is a good idea to often make him do the tasks that you know he can perform successfully, also affording you the opportunity to praise him realistically for a task well done. The young child may be able to hold his bottle by himself, later on drink from a cup, and still later help himself to a drink in the kitchen, while the older child may be able to lay the table or make tea for the rest of the family. These tasks make a child feel that he is capable, that he is important to the other members of his family, that what he does is noticed and that he has a contribution to make in his family. Note that for a young child the family represents the community. What he learns to do within the family, he will most likely also do in his community when he grows up.

5. **Tasks within his grasp.** Allow the child to successfully complete tasks that are within his ability. A child feels good when he has done something well. When he has mastered a new task successfully, allow him to do it regularly, making positive comments. By expecting a child to do something that is within his grasp, opportunities are created for the other people in his life to make positive comments.
6. **Respect.** Parents and carers are the child's role models, and by showing respect to each other, it also becomes part of the child's value system. Show your child that you respect him as well as his opinion. Say *please* and *thank you*. Treat your child and the rest of your family with the same respect that you show towards friends and strangers – they are the most important people in your life, after all. Let them see it in your daily conduct towards them.
7. **Mistakes without punishment.** Adults make many mistakes, and children should also be allowed to make mistakes without being punished for them every time. That is how they learn. Few children make mistakes on purpose, and why would they? The consequences could be quite unpleasant, after all! By correcting a child you actually say to him, *You can rely on me. I will help you. I care about you.* He interprets it as, *You love me. I am important.* For an adult, the consequences of his mistakes are usually enough punishment – the same goes for children. It should, however, be discussed with them, making them understand clearly the consequence or reaction of a particular action. This way the parent ensures that the child learns from his mistakes.
8. **Correcting behaviour.** Although behaviour should always be corrected, a child should never be humiliated. When he drops a glass of milk, for example, the parent can react in one of the following ways:
   - Lose his temper, shout and roar insults.
   - Ask him to clean up the mess.
   - Show him how to hold the glass in future so that it will not happen again – in other words, show him how to perform better physically.
   - Sigh, ignoring the child and the mess.
   - Send the child to his room.
   - Shout at someone else for allowing the child to carry the glass.

   The third choice is the best by far, reinforcing the child's positive self-image by teaching him to perform better. By developing skills, he will naturally achieve more, resulting in more praise and ultimately a better self-image. If the child is old enough to know how to clean the floor, the second choice could also be appropriate, teaching him to bear the consequences of his mistakes.

Preventing a low self-image

A good self-image can be fostered by incorporating the above-mentioned aspects into the family's daily routine. However, it is also very easy for a child to develop a poor self-image. The following are some contributing aspects that should be avoided:

1. **Contradictory behaviour** is extremely unsettling, leaving a child confused as to where he stands and what he is doing right or wrong. This happens when a parent scolds a child over a certain behaviour the one day, ignoring or even laughing about it the next. These double standards lead to feelings of insecurity and inadequacy in the child.
2. **Being insulted** is sad and upsetting for any human being, let alone a baby or child who yet has to learn where he stands with other people, who approves of him and whom he can trust. Avoid personal insults altogether, as it is often the very people who try to put themselves in a more favourable light who resort to the immature alternative of putting others in a bad light by hurling insults at them. If necessary, parents must also work on their own problems regarding poor self-image.
3. Someone who is **regularly ignored** feels that nobody notices him, that he counts for nothing and that he is not important. An ignored child often responds with negative behaviour in order to draw the attention to himself, leading to punishment or some negative reaction by adults, which further reinforces the feeling of inadequacy in the child. This can become a seriously vicious circle, so make sure that your child gets enough balanced attention from you without having to seek it through negative behaviour.
4. The **form of punishment** that a parent uses has a profound influence on the child's dignity and self-esteem. This is discussed in the chapters on parenthood and discipline.
5. Parents sometimes use **sarcasm** to 'put a child in his place'. Sarcasm, teasing and fostering guilt in a child are just as childish and unacceptable as when they are used in adult company, the difference being that adults have learned to deal or cope with this type of childishness, whereas children yet have to learn these lessons. When parents display this behaviour towards a child, it makes him feel utterly unsure of their love and support towards him, giving rise to feelings of inferiority.
6. Like all other human beings, children need space where they can freely move, play and make their own decisions. **Overprotective** parents who smother their children with attention, deny them the opportunity of learning to get along with themselves and taking control of their own small worlds. A child needs time and space to do and discover things on his own.
7. **Poor communication** among family members, and more specifically between parents and children, leads to misunderstandings and frustrations which affect both

parties. A child who does not understand the reasons for a parent's action, and then gets ignored or snubbed when he dares ask, gets the message that he is not significant or important enough to ask for or be given an explanation, once again leading to a low self-esteem.
8. Parents or carers in whom a **poor self-image** was instilled by their own parents, often find it difficult not to repeat this in their education of their children. These parents should seek professional advice in order to overcome their own poor self-image before they will be able to foster a good self-image in their children.

The role of the environment

The way a parent treats a child greatly affects the way he thinks about himself, in other words the way his self-image develops. The circumstances in which the child finds himself, and within which he grows and develops, play an equally important role in the development of a positive self-image. Optimal health enables a child to tackle problems along his way more zealously.

An environment that promotes the development of a child's individuality is also conducive to building self-image and self-esteem. Being alert to your child's natural talents, abilities and personality traits, as well as the methods that he employs to solve problems, will leave you marvelling at the way that his Creator has put him together. Appreciate his uniqueness rather than trying to cast him in a preconceived mould. Trying to force every child or family member into the same pattern will only lead to conflict in the family. Besides, it is almost impossible to change a person's natural, inborn traits – and why would anyone want to change anything that our Creator has brought about in his infinite wisdom anyway? Enjoy your child for what he is – by promoting his individuality, you are bestowing on him a precious gift.

Although the environment should offer some challenges, these challenges and demands should fall within the framework of the child's abilities. Unrealistic goals and expectations will lead to failure, resulting in a negative impact on the child's self-image.

A parent or carer who knows his child, cherishing his personality and individuality, fosters in the child a self-knowledge and self-acceptance, enabling him to discover and come to terms with both his strengths and his weaknesses within the safe environment of his family.

The environment in which a child grows up should teach him which behaviours are socially acceptable and which not. Throwing a tantrum at the age of two years may be embarrassing to the parents, but when it happens at the age of 12, it is socially unacceptable. The causes of an unsocial behaviour should be removed by the parent or carer before that behaviour becomes a habit, spoiling the child's chances of being accepted in the group. Spending time with an unmannerly child invariably results in negative reactions towards the child, giving rise to poor self-image and feelings of inadequacy in the child. Help your child by reacting to his unsocial behaviour without delay. Children sometimes act in a rude and unsocial manner without realising that it is wrong. Not understanding why people react negatively towards them, they come to the logical, but wrongful, conclusion that they are unloved.

Socially accepted behaviour also plays a role in the ability to build relationships with other people. A child must learn that he cannot think of himself only, but that other people's feelings and desires should also be considered. If this principle is instilled in a child from a young age, and also adhered to by the parent, it should pave the way for a happy, healthy relationship between them, resulting in largely unproblematic teenage years. Teach the very young child to share – give him two sweets instead of one, for example, encouraging him to give one away, even to a pet or a doll if there is no-one else around! Talk about other people's feelings, teaching your child to appreciate their position. When you come across a beggar, for instance, discuss the situation with your child, talking about the beggar's world at a level that the child will understand. This way he learns that other people's worlds and needs may differ radically from his own. The ability to see and understand a situation from someone else's perspective is the first step towards good interpersonal relations.

Parents and carers should be aware of these practical ways in which their child's most precious possession – a positive self-image – can be cherished and enhanced.

The development of play

Play involves any activity pursued solely for enjoyment and repeated entirely for the delight of the player. It happens voluntarily, involving no external pressure whatsoever.

However, for a child, to play means to work. It is his way of learning and gaining experience. As has been explained in previous chapters, through play, a young child acquires numerous skills. The same applies to the older child – when playing 'mom/dad' or 'teacher', not only does he experience pleasure, but he also *becomes* the mom/dad or teacher. When the child plays, he reacts, trying out and practising the careers, skills and customs that he perceives in the world around him, preparing himself for the life ahead of him.

Stages of play

As with any other skill, play develops following a specific pattern, with the child passing through different stages as he gets older. Although the stages follow a fixed sequence, the child constantly reverts to earlier stages as well. After an illness or other trauma the child sometimes regresses to a previous stage of development, also with regards to play. The development stages of play can be summarised as follows:

- **Uninvolved play:** The child is not involved in any task yet, being concerned with the satisfaction of his own physical needs only.
- **Solitary play:** The child plays alone with himself (e.g. his fingers or toes) or with his toys. Interaction with others happens for emotional reasons only and does not take place during play.
- **Spectator play:** The child watches other children play, without getting involved himself.
- **Imitating play:** The child watches other children or adults, imitating their behaviour. This is an important method of learning, teaching social skills, cultural aspects, vocabulary and table manners, among other things. As this is a powerful, highly effective way of learning and playing, parents should be mindful of the example that they, and other people, set for the child. If you do not want your child to swear, you must refrain from swearing yourself, or he will no doubt pick it up – and if you reprimand the child, you deserve an even sharper reprimand yourself! Protect your baby or child against people who set a bad example by avoiding their company. There is a good reason why TV programs and movies have an age restriction – decide if you agree with it, then stick to it.
- **Constructive play:** The child starts, and completes, a task in order to construct or create an end product. Babies and toddlers, being more task-orientated, are seldom interested in an end product, deriving satisfaction from participation in the task rather than the end product. The older child, on the other hand, takes great pride in a successfully executed task, which can be anything from washing his own face to completing a jigsaw puzzle. The end product (in this case either a clean face or a completed jigsaw puzzle) is usually achieved by following specific rules or steps in a particular order.
- **Parallel play:** Two children play the same game next to each other (each with his own toy car, for example), making little observable contact. They are, however, aware of each other, enjoying the other's presence.
- **Communal play:** Two or more children take part in the same activity, making contact and communicating with one another, but not working together towards the same goal. They may, for example, play together with a ball, but there are no rules involved and turns can only be taken under adult guidance.
- **Cooperative play:** Two or more children play (or work) together towards the same goal, for example, icing a cake or building a 'farm' in the mud. They follow the rules or make their own rules which need to be observed in order to reach their collective goal.
- **Competitive play:** Two or more children take part in the same activity, with the purpose of beating the others and performing better than the rest, for example, running a race or playing a game with the aim to win.
- **Creative play:** The child participates in a task where he discovers a new way of using the material, creates his own new rules for a game, or does something that

he has not been taught before, thereby employing his creative ability to make a new discovery. This type of play can happen alone or in a group. When a group is involved, either the creative idea of one group member is used to perform the task, or it inspires more creative ideas from other group members, combining creative and cooperative play.
- **Fantasy play:** Although fantasy is a form of creative play, there is no connection with reality, making it unsuitable for application in daily life. However vital for the promotion of creative thought, in order to be creative, the dream world of fantasy has to be integrated with reality. For example, the child fantasises about the potential of a wooden block that is used as a car. Only when he puts the block on wheels and draws windows on the sides to make it look like a car, does this become creative play.

As we already know, the stages of play follow sequentially as the child develops. A young baby is in the uninvolved stage of play, progressively passing through the other stages as he gets older. Once again, no specific ages are linked to the stages, as children gradually progress from one to the next, sometimes reverting to previous stages and then quickly progressing to the rest. A rough indication is that a baby is mostly in the uninvolved stage of play, starting with parallel play by about one year of age, while cooperative play takes place under adult guidance from around two to three years and four-year-olds are mostly in the fantasy stage. As a balanced child uses all different stages of play during his development (and even sometimes into adulthood, as you will see later on), no stage of play can be regarded more important than another.

Analysing your child's stage of play as he is playing is rather interesting, giving you much more insight when problems arise, and being particularly helpful when coming across, and having to deal with, difficult situations. For example, when two girls are playing dolls and one complains about the other, it is good to know that they are using cooperative play, but that the rules have not been set out clearly. If the parent can help to clear that up, the conflict can usually be dissolved, allowing play to continue. On the other hand, two babies may be fighting over the same toy. When considering their stage of play, you will realise that they have not reached the cooperative stage yet and so cannot apply rules. For your own peace of mind and for the sake of harmony, it is easier to give both of them the same toy and simply remove the toy that has caused the fight.

A child who is sick or tired is usually quite happy to be a spectator as other children play, or to watch television. For the particular child, this 'passiveness' is also a type of play (namely spectator play) which can be very satisfying. So, when a child has an extended illness or is somehow physically restrained from taking part in normal play, the parent can rest assured that he still enjoys other children's company, even though he joins in as a spectator only.

At times these stages are also observed in adult behaviour – although we do not call them 'play', they are closely related to the stages that children go through:

- **Uninvolved play:** We become quiet, reflect, retreat from the world or go for a solitary walk.
- **Solitary play:** We work alone or practise a solitary hobby.
- **Spectator play:** We watch television, attend a sports match or go to the theatre.
- **Imitating play:** Although adults do not consciously imitate others, the success of advertisements is frequently aimed at our habit of doing what the people around us do. Being imitators by nature, we use this type of play more often than we would care to admit, sometimes in a positive, and other times in a negative, manner.
- **Constructive play:** The construction of an object is done according to specific steps or rules – this may be anything from building a jigsaw puzzle to building a house.
- **Parallel play:** Although we share an office with other people and are aware of our colleagues' presence, each of us performs our own task at our own desk.
- **Communal play:** We attend a social function, or take part in a sport such as walking or cycling – each at his own tempo and without competing, albeit along the same route.
- **Cooperative play:** We take part in a team sport, or work together in a group in order to complete a task and reach a common goal.
- **Competitive play:** Although we take part in the same task or sport, our goal is to perform better than the others in order to win the competition.
- **Creative play:** We make a plan or solve a problem by using a new, innovative method.
- **Fantasy play:** We daydream or fantasise about a book or a movie, often initiating a creative process.

Paying attention to, and regularly utilising, these stages of play benefit adults, not only by bringing them joy and satisfaction, but also by helping them to become more balanced human beings who spend sufficient time with their own thoughts, with their friends, at work and in a team, as well as competing, daydreaming and planning creatively.

Remember, once again, that children are preparing for the adult life. If any one of these stages is skipped or does not receive enough attention, there will be voids in the adult's life, giving rise to maladjustment, unhappiness or rebelliousness, poor interpersonal relations, poor social adaptation skills or selective emotional maturity.

Aspects that influence play

The same aspects that influence our daily functioning and performance, also affect children's play. They are:

- **Health.** Nobody can zealously participate in a task when feeling sick or listless.
- **Previous experience.** When a child is introduced to a new task, he must be guided and supported until he has gained enough understanding to master it by himself.
- **Motor skill.** A child who has not developed enough skill to master a task, will either withdraw or perform poorly. Here age should also be taken into account – tell your child that the reason why his friend performs better at a specific task, is because he is older.
- **Gender.** The child's gender and identification with an adult have an important impact on his or her choice of play and toys. For example, a boy pretends to be shaving like his dad, while a girl imitates her mom polishing her nails.
- **Environment.** Because play is often imitating, environmental events are an important source of imitation. The environment also determines the availability of equipment, the place where the child plays and the accessibility of playmates. Some children have access to a fully-equipped playroom, while others have to settle for the stones and earth next to a maize field.
- **Time.** Make time for play, otherwise a whole day may pass during which the child only follows instructions and obeys commands without any opportunity for spontaneous and innovative *play*.

Children who find themselves in a stimulating environment where play is cherished and encouraged, are keen to learn new games and acquire new skills. These include social skills and emotional lessons. A child who is stimulated and encouraged to explore and learn about his environment, is seldom bored. A keen interest in his environment enables the child to occupy himself creatively and constructively, not only affording his parents some time for themselves, but also allowing the child to develop into an adult who can keep himself busy, refraining from all sorts of wrong practices resulting from boredom. A child who can play, either alone or with friends, is usually a happy child who has already taken the first steps to a happy adulthood.

Speech and language development

The helplessness of a newborn baby is largely due to his inability to convey his needs in a way that other people can understand. This helplessness quickly diminishes during the early years as the baby gains better control of the muscles used for the various communication mechanisms or speech organs.

The ability to talk also affects another important aspect of the child's life, namely his need to belong to a social group. Communication among group members is imperative for belonging to a group and for acceptance as a group member.

As with other areas of development, the early years are critical for the development of speech. The foundation for future speech development is laid during babyhood. Also, it is possible to make compensation for early speech problems later on, and although ineffective speech patterns can be rectified, the foundation laid during early babyhood has a permanent effect on a child's speech pattern.

As a toddler needs to be physically and intellectually ready for speech, it is important to have a good role model whom he can imitate, as well as ample opportunity to practise his speech skills. Encouraging your baby to talk, and giving him the correct guidance, will help him to establish good speech habits.

The following are the most important skills that a child needs to acquire in order to develop decent speech:

- building a good vocabulary
- correct pronunciation of words
- the ability to use the different words in a grammatically correct sentence

A child who hears little speech, or is often exposed to incorrect language usage (e.g. from a carer who cannot speak his mother tongue fluently), is more prone to language and speech problems than a child who hears proper speech and language all day long and receives the right guidance, at the right time, for acquiring language.

Good speech habits afford a baby, toddler or child the opportunity to articulate his own needs and to make himself better understood by the people around him, ensuring that they pay attention to him and that his social needs are met. A good vocabulary enables a child to understand other people's language and to be taught basic social concepts from a young age. Good language and speech may even empower the child to influence other people's behaviour, thoughts and feelings, making them important social skills to acquire.

Pre-speech communication

Learning to talk is a long and complicated process. As the child grows and develops, he uses different methods of communication in order to make himself understood. This is called 'pre-speech'. Pre-speech communication contributes to shortening a baby's helpless period dramatically. This type of communication is used until the child's language ability has developed to such an extent that he can use meaningful words that are understood by himself and by other people.

During the first 18 months of the baby's life, or until he has acquired enough vocabulary to make verbal communication possible, four types of pre-speech communication are employed:
- crying
- babbling
- gesturing
- emotional expression

As far as speech development is concerned, **babbling** is the most important of these four, laying the foundation for proper speech. These basic sounds, which are incidentally generated by movements of the vocal organs, depend largely on the shape of the oral cavity and the way in which it modifies the airflow from the lungs passing over the vocal chords. These sounds are not acquired and are the same in all babies, including deaf babies. Although many of the initial cooing sounds disappear, some develop into babbling and later into words. However, this is regarded as play rather than communication, giving the baby a great amount of pleasure.

The number of sounds gradually increases, as does the clarity of the various sounds. True babbling is 'mah-mah-mah-mah' or 'ugh-ugh'. As the baby learns to control the air flow over his vocal chords, voluntary sounds are produced. Although babbling can be regarded as voluntary vocal gymnastics, there is no semantic value involved.

The amount of babbling, and the time that it takes to merge into speech, are largely influenced by the degree to which a baby is encouraged to babble. A baby who is babbled *to* and given new models to imitate, not only babbles, but also learns to use a wider variety of babbling sounds than a baby who receives no stimulation in this regard.

Babbling increases the need to communicate with others. Babies frequently try to become involved in a conversation between two people by babbling while they talk. The increase in the amount of babbling when being talked to is another clear indication of a baby's attempt to communicate.

Babbling further serves to make a baby feel part of a social group. This feeling intensifies when group members talk to the baby or babble in reaction to her babbling. Feeling part of a social group prevents a feeling of social isolation, which could hinder communication.

Gestures are limb movements which either serve as substitutes for speech or to supplement speech, conveying thoughts or emotions through meaningful movements rather than words. Unlike babbling, which is principally regarded as a form of play, gesturing can be used as a satisfactory substitute for speech until the baby learns to use words, and as such, can be regarded as a medium of communication. Children use gesturing to complete their sentences until their vocabulary allows them to express their needs, thoughts, desires and feelings in words. As the child's speech improves, the need for gesturing diminishes.

In order to ease communication between them, a parent or carer can teach a baby a range of gestures, empowering him to indicate his need by means of a specific gesture, and obviating the need for screaming or crying whenever a need arises. The parent can either interpret, expand and encourage the baby's own gestures, or teach the baby existing 'sign language' (see www.babyhands.co.za, www.signlanguageforbaby.com and www.tinytalk.com.au), enabling him to communicate with the parent by means of gestures until he has learned to use words. Babies enjoy this manner of 'talking' and announcing their needs. Using the same gestures, the parent also verbalises them, thereby expanding the baby's language and vocabulary.

The following are some common gestures used by most babies, which parents should soon learn to understand:

Gesture:	Meaning:
Allowing food to run from mouth	Content or not hungry
Spitting	Discontented
Pushing breast/teat out with tongue	Content or not hungry
Pushing object away	Not wanting it

Gesture:	Meaning:
Reaching for object	Wanting it
Reaching for a person	Wanting to be picked up
Smacking lips or protruding tongue	Hungry
Smiling or extending arms	Wanting to be picked up
Sneezing repeatedly	Wet and cold
Squirming and trembling	Cold
Squirming while bathing or changing	Fighting restriction of movements
Turning head away from breast/teat	Content or not hungry

The older baby soon learns to shake his head to indicate that he is not interested in whatever he is being offered. An observant parent can look out for more gestures, encouraging the baby to use them as 'sign language' – for example, lifting his arm for 'stop' and extending his hand for 'give'. Various gestures for basic verbs and nouns serve as a communication medium that diminishes frustration in both the parent and the baby. This works well until the age of two or three years, after which it is replaced with the numerous words that the baby learns to say.

During the pre-speech period, a baby uses body positions and facial expressions to show his **emotions**. Pleasant emotions are accompanied by pleasant sounds such as cooing and laughter, together with relaxed arm and leg movements, while anger is expressed by tenseness in the body, kicking and boxing of the legs and arms, a strained look on the face and crying.

Before a baby learns to control his emotions, his uncontrolled behaviour allows the parent to know how he feels about people and situations. Babies also have the ability to interpret other people's emotional expressions, quickly noticing a change in facial expression and tone of voice. Although he may not understand the meaning of the words, "That is naughty", the baby can gather from the facial expression and the tone of voice that the person who talks to him is not happy.

As with gesturing, emotional expression remains a useful method of communication, even after the child has learned to talk. Because emotions are more difficult to verbalise, emotional expression is employed more frequently than gesturing.

Vocabulary

A baby's vocabulary expands as he becomes older, gaining control of his speech organs and becoming more motivated to talk. The first words that a child uses are nouns – usually single syllables merging from his favourite babbling sounds. Once he knows enough nouns to name people and objects in his environment, he starts using verbs, especially those that describe actions, such as *'give'*, *'take'* and *'hold'*. From around 18 months of age, adjectives appear in the child's vocabulary, the most common ones being *'good'*, *'bad'*, *'pretty'*, *'naughty'*, *'hot'* and *'cold'*, mostly used with regard to people, food and toys. Adverbs develop simultaneously with adjectives, the first ones usually being *'here'* and *'there'*. Possessive pronouns are last in line, being the most difficult to use. Because young children are confused by *'I'*, *'my'* and *'mine'*, the use of these pronouns are postponed for as long as possible, being replaced with the child's own name instead. Children's speech is either egocentric (talking about themselves) or socialised (talking about other people), egocentric speech being increasingly replaced with socialised speech as the child grows older.

Parents often complain that a toddler in the question stage cries when the parent says *'no'*, sometimes putting the parent in a difficult spot. Before saying *'no'*, the situation should be considered very carefully. While your ultimate message may still mean *'no'*, it should be put in a more positive way, for example, "Playtime is up, we have to go. Do you want to walk or shall I carry you?" If the child still cries or whines when you have to leave, firmly say, "It is okay if you want to cry – I know you feel sad because we have to go now. But it is getting late and we cannot stay longer." Do not give in to the child's request to stay longer, as he quickly learns that crying or whining will get him his way, encouraging him to manipulate the parent from a young age. The same applies when he wants a toy or sweet in the shop – let him cry and do not give in. The child soon learns that his whining serves no purpose and that he simply has to obey.

Around the age of two years, toddlers often display a dramatic development in their use of language. Their vocabulary expands drastically, as do their usage of grammar and their ability to understand sentence construction. This is when the endless questions begin, starting with simply calling the parent – over and over and over again! The questions gradually become more complex, including, "Where?" and "Why?", for example, and reaching a peak between the ages of 2½ and 3½ years. The questions, usually involving people, places and objects in the toddler's environment, but in reality referring to his own fears, concerns and interests, are aimed at trying to understand the people and the world around him. While babies are only interested in their own physical needs, the questions toddlers ask are aimed at getting to know the world around them better and faster. Repeating the same questions over and over, and hearing the same answers time after time serve as assurance that he has heard correctly and make the toddler feel secure.

Promotion of language and listening skills

During the question stage, the parents' response to the toddler's questions is particularly important for his motivation to learn and explore, as well as for his development of a healthy self-image. When parents get angry or become irritated with the endless questions that a toddler asks, they convey the message that he should suppress his need to learn and explore in order to appease the people whom he loves. This leads to a passive acceptance of his world and circumstances, rather than becoming an active, dynamic role player.

The following are methods that can be used for improving your child's language and listening skills:

- Talk to your child as often as possible – he understands much more than he can show or say. The more you talk, the better the example that he gets from you and the sooner he will start to imitate you.
- Make eye contact when your child talks to you, showing genuine interest in what he has to say. Listen attentively, as the information that he conveys is important to him. Your full attention also motivates the child to talk, making him feel that it is worthwhile talking to you.
- A child asks questions to expand his knowledge, your answers being the exact information that your child needs at that moment.
- The speech that children hear at home has a greater impact on them than only learning it at school. Make an effort to use interesting and creative language, often reading aloud about different subjects, singing, reading nursery rhymes and poems, and using an interesting and extended vocabulary.
- When you take your child on an outing, talk to him and encourage him to talk to you too, albeit only babbling at first – the words and narratives will follow later. Imitate sounds, words and stories that you come across during your outings.
- Talk about the tasks that you perform every day, why you do them and what exactly you are doing. Help your child to understand the world around him, but also to verbalise it so that other people will understand him.
- Read to your child every day, making stories an important and enjoyable part of your daily routine. This is one of the most valuable sources of language acquisition.
- Employ as many senses as possible when teaching your child a new word or concept.
- Ask your child questions, encouraging him to answer or react. An older child can be encouraged to describe, or give a detailed account of objects or events.

The development of speech and language is closely related to the development of a baby's auditory abilities, in other words, her hearing and her interpretation of what she hears. In this chapter you have constantly been reminded of the importance of talking to your baby, giving her something to listen to. What is equally important, however, is that she will learn to understand what she is listening to, a process that happens simultaneously with the acquisition of language. This means that the games described under 'Sense of hearing' in chapter 5 will also serve to stimulate your baby's language development.

11

Perceptual and cognitive development

Perceptual development

Perceptual development is the development of various perceptions of the world and the environment in which the child finds himself, in other words, the experience or the idea that the child has of objects and events in his environment. Varying from person to person, perceptions can also change according to circumstances. For example, one person may think that the sea has a pink glow at sunset, while another observes it as orange. Or one person may think that music is loud and noisy, while another regards it as exciting rock. They have different perceptions. A perception is influenced by a person's observation (the messages that his senses send to his brain), as well as his previous experiences (the nerve tracts and synapses that have already stabilised). The first time that a baby hears loud march music, he may perceive it as alarming and start crying, whereas by the tenth time he may associate it with pleasant memories of his parents' good humour when listening to it, causing him to laugh excitedly.

Efficient perceptual development is dependent on efficient stimulation of the sensory systems. Well-developed visual and auditory perceptual abilities are imperative for coping with academic tasks in the formal school, laying the foundation for the proper observation of colour, shape and size (which may have an important effect on handwriting and reading ability), as well as for language, speech and hearing (which may greatly affect reading ability, vocabulary, sentence construction and the following of instructions). Children with well-developed perceptual abilities usually perform better at school than children who experience problems in this regard.

As this book is focused mainly on the first three years of a child's development, preparation for formal schooling is not discussed here. A toddler whose sensory and motor development is stimulated, should not experience any problems with perceptual development. However, parents should not hesitate to consult a professional person, such as an occupational therapist specialising in child development and learning difficulties, regarding their children's development. Potential problems can be dealt with very successfully if they are detected early enough, before the commencement of formal schooling.

Although the formation of concepts can be observed in many different fields, as far as visual-perceptual concepts of shapes and the reproduction of shapes are concerned, the development of a child's drawings may be observed. Just as a child babbles before he talks, he scribbles before he writes or starts to make decent drawings. And just as the child's babbling should be encouraged in order to stimulate speech and language, his scribbling should also be encouraged in order to stimulate writing and drawing.

The scribbling phase is an important phase of development, stretching from around 16 months to around four years of age. Even a five-year-old will scribble if that is the first time that he is given the opportunity to draw. The scribbling phase can be divided into three stages:

- Uncontrolled scribbling:

These are the first random marks that the toddler makes with a drawing tool (pencil, crayon or paintbrush).

- Controlled scribbling:

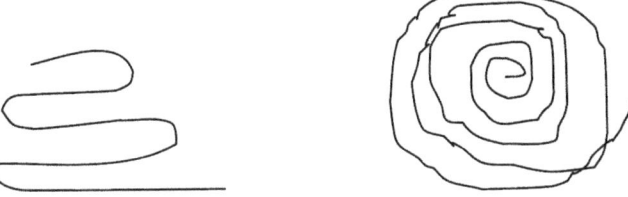

Approximately six months after the child's first attempts at scribbling, he discovers that there is a connection between the movement that he makes with his hand and the mark left on the paper. He now gains control of his scribbling, repeating it intentionally. He tries to stay on the paper or board that is given to him, for the fist time making use of space and developing an understanding of space on paper.

The child also starts labelling his scribbled pattern (calling it a ball, for example), using his context of the world to make a mark on the paper and realising that it can be given a name. This is the first time that he makes use of a symbol (which is the first step to reading and writing). Giving a child pictures to colour in or to copy has no developmental value whatsoever, depriving the child of the opportunity to get a grasp of this concept of symbols.

- Early symbols:

In this stage, the child starts to use his scribbling to make intentional shapes. By approximately three years of age, he begins to combine circles and lines, using them as symbols that represent objects. Because humans are the most significant objects in the child's world, that is what he normally draws first and, also, most frequently.

Initially the humans in the child's drawings do not have torsos – this is quite normal, being done by children of all population groups throughout the world, not because the child does not know that a person has a torso, but because the head and body are perceived as one. A young child will also use any colour, for example blue hair, even though he knows that people do not have blue hair. It is simply not of any importance to him.

Because a young child has not developed a concept of perspective, his drawings of people make them look as if they hang in the air. He may also turn the paper, starting to draw from any corner. Do not tell the child that this is wrong – as his perception and perspective develop, so will his drawings. Also, do not teach a child how to draw a specific object – his drawings will develop in proportion to the development of his perceptual abilities.

Cognitive development

Cognitive development is the development of the ability to 'use one's brains' – the ability to think, reason, remember and make adjustments in order to function efficiently. Good cognitive abilities are associated with intelligence and success, not only at school, but also in the rest of a person's life.

Cognitive functioning has many aspects, of which only the following three are discussed in this chapter:
- creative development
- conceptual development
- moral development

Creativity

Creativity is a person's ability to come up with new or innovative plans and ideas, involving the formation of new thought patterns, new combinations of previously acquired information, and the application of old ideas to new situations, leading to the formation of new ideas. Creativity is purpose-driven, having a specific end product in mind. Although it does not always have immediate value and the product is not instantly completed and perfected, creativity is not just a vague vision, but has the potential to develop into a functional and practical end product. This may be in the form of a piece of art, a work of literature or a scientific invention, but it may also be a process. A creative person is not, as many people suggest, the absent-minded artist who never achieves anything. A truly creative person solves problems by employing new ways of thinking, by lateral thoughts and by refusal to conform. It is creative people who, by their ability to think ahead and plan proactively, think of new ways to ensure not only the continued existence of the earth, but also of every small group or enterprise.

Creative people usually have a combination of qualities that includes adaptability, flexibility, nonconformity, independence, high personal expectations, discipline, the ability to play around with ideas, self-confidence, a sense of humour, curiosity, a predilection for fantasy, a preference for choosing their own interests, and many more.

These qualities can hardly be stimulated by playing specific games with a child. Rather, stimulating creativity involves establishing a milieu within which creative thought is encouraged. From as early as the toddler stage, your child can be motivated to think laterally by encouraging him to come up with his own solutions to a difficult task, for instance, rather than showing or teaching him straight away. Although the correct or a better method, can still be taught in a positive way – after the child has been encouraged to think creatively – parents should guard against a destructive response to the child's own solution.

For example, when your toddler whinges as he is trying to carry a big doll, he should be encouraged to come up with a solution. Start by verbalising the problem: "You have difficulty carrying the doll, because it is very big and heavy." Then ask him what solution he has in mind: "What do you think we can do to make it easier?" Listen, and look at his solution. Never say, "No, that won't work." Rather say, "Yes, that's a good idea. What else can we do?" If you have time and the child is not too impatient, you can make a silly game of it: "Yes, we can put the doll in Daddy's car, or you can drag the doll instead of carrying it, or I can carry the doll for you, or we can tie the doll to your back, or we can cut the doll into pieces and you can carry it one piece at a time, or we can leave the doll right here and let it sleep – she looks tired, or ..." and so you can carry on, laughing over all the silly suggestions and eventually deciding on the best solution. Apart from teaching your child to think laterally, he also learns that problems usually have more than one solution.

The value of creativity is too great to be ignored. Be alert to the creative qualities in your child, encouraging him to become a creative person and not allowing your actions and responses to inhibit his creativity. The following are some of the numerous advantages that creativity holds for a person:

- The creative process brings personal joy and satisfaction. Few things give greater pleasure to a child than creating something himself. Similarly, few things are more destructive to a child's self-image than when the created product is criticised or misunderstood.
- Creativity adds joy to a young child's play. Children who are encouraged to express their creativity are happy and content.
- Creative activities allow children to achieve success in areas that are important to them. The positive reaction of the important people in the child's life builds a good self-image.
- Figuring strongly in leadership, creativity helps a child to become a leader in his group. New ideas for play are popular among group members.
- All the above aspects of creativity are inducive to personal and social adaptation.

To prevent a child from becoming an unpractical dreamer, creative thoughts should be converted into practical actions wherever possible. A balance should be maintained between creativity leading to practical problem solving, and fantasy without any practical implication.

Creativity starts very early in a child's life, finding expression in his manner of play. As he gets older, it also develops in other areas of his life, such as his schoolwork, sports, recreation and, eventually, also his career. Teach your child to play with simple objects, encouraging him to use his imagination. Make a game of simple activities, such as shaking teaspoons in a saucepan to make 'music', looking at pictures in a book, dancing to the beat of music and thinking of silly solutions to problems – teaching the child to find joy in relatively simple play. This way he also learns that he has the ability to control and successfully manipulate objects in his environment, as well as the environment itself, to a certain degree. On the other hand, parents who inhibit creativity teach their child that objects in the environment should rather be left untouched, as they may be dangerous or evoke a negative response from the parent, depriving the child of the self-confidence to manipulate his environment. Although every child has the potential to be creative, that creativity can only be expanded and developed if the environment is inducive to creative development.

Environmental aspects that promote creativity include the following:

- Ample free time
- Opportunities for solitary play (play apart from a group or other family members promotes a rich imagination)
- Encouragement of creativity and abstention from criticism (which inhibits creativity)
- Availability of equipment that motivates the child to experiment
- A stimulating environment that guides and motivates the child to use the available equipment, from his baby days throughout his school years
- A healthy parent-child relationship that promotes independence by not overprotecting the child
- A democratic parent who encourages creativity, as opposed to an authoritarian parent who inhibits creativity (more about this in chapter 13)
- Opportunities for expansion of knowledge (a wide knowledge and experience lay the foundation for creative processes)

The parent should be alert to the creativity finding expression in the toddler's play, encouraging and channelling it to develop from dream and fantasy to practical problem solving. A baby starts manipulating toys from a very young age, deriving great pleasure from applying the same object in different ways. A young child may identify with a toy, such as a doll, giving her her first opportunity to put herself in someone else's position. The child projects her own emotions onto the doll, so that the doll also has an 'owie', for example. These are the first lessons in sympathy and empathy. Events and people in the child's environment, as well as in the media, are employed as creative themes during imitating and dramatic play.

Humour is a fun form of creativity that involves both the ability to see the comical in a situation and to create a comical situation. Because people enjoy being in the company of a humourous person, both aspects of humour contribute to the social acceptance of that person. Humour requires constructing new perceptions and employing funny ways to link them with previous experiences. Although the ability to make others laugh is generally inducive to self-confidence and a good self-image in children, using that ability to put others in a bad light leads to social rejection, giving rise to poor personal adaptation.

Stories are an excellent source of creativity. The first stories that a child tells are merely a verbal reproduction of events conveyed by the child, initially making use of a very limited vocabulary, which expands in proportion as he is encouraged to tell more stories. Stories that are told to the child, or that he sees or hears in the media, give him an opportunity to repeat, or reproduce, the story. As he becomes more creative, he makes up stories based on his own experiences and on what he sees and hears in the media, adding a good dash of his own original ideas. At this stage, a parent will have to exercise good power of judgment in order to discriminate between lies and original ideas deserving of encouragement. Using creativity to add flavour to a story or to stimulate a young child's imagination is good, but when a child uses creativity to avoid punishment or to put others in a bad light, the parent should explain the consequences to him, nipping it in the bud.

There is no way of measuring creative potential in a young child. What we do know, however, is that creativity is often inhibited in children in an effort to shape them into the persons that their parents and communities expect them to be. As creativity can never really be suppressed, however, it always finds expression in some way or other. If a child is not guided or allowed to channel this creativity in a positive way, it may find expression in rebelliousness and socially unaccepted behaviour patterns.

Conceptual ability

Conceptual ability is the ability to understand with insight, applying previous knowledge and experiences to new situations. The adjustments that children make in their lives are greatly influenced by the conception that they have of their environment, of the people in their environment and of themselves. A child who understands the dangers posed by a motor vehicle will be mindful in the presence of moving vehicles, while a child who does not understand the dangers, will not take ample precautions to prevent an accident, leading to inappropriate adjustment responses which could be hazardous to the child. Children who do not have a conception of their own abilities and inabilities, do not understand why people respond to them in a certain way, resulting in possible misinterpretations of other people's intentions.

A child's attitude towards other people and various aspects in his environment, as well as his perception of what is important in life, depends on his conception of the world around him. One of the greatest benefits of understanding the world around you is an ability to adapt to that world, personally as well as environmentally.

As we have seen in previous chapters, when a baby is born, he has no understanding of his environment whatsoever, yet having to form a conception of the world. As he becomes older and more mature, he learns through new experiences to understand the various aspects of his environment. As the environment becomes more meaningful to him, he begins to understand himself in relation to his environment. The parent is in the privileged position of helping his child getting to understand his environment, enabling him to control it with confidence and responsibility.

Good cognitive development is necessary in order to enable a child to form conceptions. Piaget described two primary periods, divided into four stages, for the development of cognitive function. Being subdivisions of the same process that forms a continuous pattern of cognitive development, these stages cannot be separated.

- The first period is the **period of sensory-motor development**, divided into the senso-motor and preoperational stages. During the senso-motor stage, which stretches from birth to around two years of age, the child develops a conception of himself apart from the environment. The preoperational stage, which roughly stretches from two to six years, is the stage of imaginative play and egocentric thoughts, during which the child starts to use language and symbolic thinking.
- The second period is the **period of conceptual development**, divided into the stages of concrete and formal operations. During the stage of concrete operations, which stretches from six to around 12 years of age, the child starts to form conceptions of various environmental aspects, including space, time and the ability to categorise objects. Although the book is not focused on this age group, it is mentioned here to stress the importance of a rich and stimulating environment for the child's eventual adaptability as an adult. The same applies to the stage of formal operations, which stretches from around 12 years to adulthood, during which the child explores different methods of problem solving, already having mastered hypothetic reasoning.

Maturity provides a basis for conceptual readiness. In other words, the child's brain, nervous system, sensory organs, and ability to observe and to form perceptions, have to develop and reach maturity before his conceptual ability can reach maturity. Once again, the development and functioning of the advanced, complex functions are dependent on the earlier, simpler processes of growth and development.

Conceptual ability not only enables the child to see the relation between new and previous experiences, but also provides him with a way to understand and efficiently adapt to his environment.

The abilities to learn from old and new experiences, and to make associations, depends on the ability to form environmental conceptions. Conceptions are not direct sensory information, but are formed as a result of an extension and combination, (or merging), of specific sensory experiences. Conceptions are symbolic, depending on the qualities of both absent and present situations and objects, and often contain an emotional component that becomes part of the conception, determining how the child feels about, and reacts to, the situation or object.

Conceptions are complex relations, changing continually as a child develops and gains experience and new information and knowledge. Conceptions are formed of objects or relations and situations, and cannot always be put into words. Although a child may have a clear and accurate conception of what 'dishonesty' means, for example, he may not have the vocabulary to describe it. Conceptions are important in that they determine what we know and believe and ultimately also, to a large extent, what we do.

A child's understanding is influenced by the accuracy of his conceptions. The more conceptions a child has, and the more developed and accurate they are, the better his understanding. As the baby is exposed to all the objects and events in his environment, perceptions are formed that merge with previous perceptions, resulting in the formation of conceptions.

The following are some aspects that are imperative for the promotion of conceptual development in children:

1. The ability to see the relation between new and previous experiences. Development of this ability starts before the baby's first birthday, after which it rapidly accelerates. As the child grows older, and new experiences have increasingly more in common with existing knowledge and experiences, these connections become easier to grasp.
2. The ability to perceive the underlying meaning of a situation. Children perceive objects, people and the environment as they see them, learning only much later to perceive what cannot be seen.
3. The ability to reason and think creatively. This is necessary for the accurate observation and interpretation of situations. Even older children, and sometimes also adults, may have difficulty with this, giving rise to misunderstandings.

So, like most other abilities, the ability to form and understand conceptions starts developing during the baby years. This development continues throughout a person's life, even into adulthood, and can be expanded and sharpened until a high age. Exposing a child to a stimulating environment with numerous experiences, old as well as new, promotes the development of insight, knowledge and concept formation, resulting in greater responsibility, a better understanding of his environment and consequently better performance. This goes hand-in-hand with the development of a positive self-image, which is further boosted by the child's mature behaviour in various situations, and forms the foundation for an integrated, balanced human being with a keen insight – a great gift to the community in which the child grows up.

Moral values

Moral behaviour is behaviour that complies with the moral code of the social group and is determined by moral conceptions, in other words, the rules of conduct that group members follow customarily, and that are also the expectation of the group for its members. Moral behaviour becomes a custom before it develops into a culture. Immoral behaviour does not result from ignorance of the culture, but rather from an aversion to the group standards or a reluctance to conform.

Amoral behaviour, on the other hand, usually resulting from ignorance of the culture or the group's expectations, is not a deliberate breach of the culture. Unacceptable behaviour by young children can be regarded as amoral rather than immoral.

As no child is born with a set of values or rules of conduct, all newborn babies can be considered amoral. Children cannot be expected to develop a moral code by themselves – they need someone to teach them the group standard and the difference between right and wrong. The process of learning to behave in a socially acceptable way is a long and slow road, starting in the baby years and continuing into adolescence. This is one of the most important developmental tasks during childhood. Before a child reaches school age, he should already have learned the difference between right and wrong in simple situations, and have developed a conscience. Before his childhood is over, the child should possess a set of values, together with an appropriate conscience, guiding him to make decisions in accordance with moral principles. In order to develop a moral code, a child has to learn the following:
- what the expectations of his social group are
- the ability to feel guilt and shame
- what the group members' expectations are during interaction with one another

Each social group, or culture, has laws accompanied by appropriate penalties should those laws be violated, as well as customs which are not specifically punished when they are infringed upon. Parents, teachers and carers should guide and help children to conform to the group's accepted patterns of behaviour by laying down rules, and equipping them with prescribed behaviour patterns.

This is a mouthful and although it may not seem applicable to babies and young children, that is exactly where many parents make the mistake. Babies grow older and have to live within a specific culture when they grow up – therefore they need to be taught from babyhood that some things are taboo and will be punished. Although overly strict discipline and severe punishment are once again unacceptable, children must know what is right and what is wrong. A child who does not behave in accordance with the moral code of his culture and social group, is unpopular – people's reactions to his behaviour destroying his self-image in various respects. If the child does not know right from wrong, he will not be able to understand why people react to him in this way.

The acquisition of moral principles involves, among other things, the development of an inner conscience that controls the child's behaviour. Experts agree that children are not born with a conscience and a knowledge of right and wrong – these have to be acquired. As it is too difficult for a young child to acquire this conscience based on the moral values of the group, his behaviour has to be controlled by the environment in which he finds himself. As the child grows older, there is a shift from environmental control to inner control over his own behaviour. For example, when a young baby hits a little friend, he often simply needs to be removed from the friend in order to put an end to the behaviour (environmental control). As he grows older, however, he develops a conscience, realising by himself that it is wrong to hit the friend (inner control). After the development of his conscience, the child feels guilty and/or ashamed when he fails to behave in accordance with the norm. Social interaction plays an important role in moral development, the group's approval or disapproval of the behaviour serving as a guideline for socially accepted behaviour, motivating the child to behave accordingly.

A child's first social interactions take place within the family group, where the group values, as well as the difference between right and wrong, are conveyed by parents, siblings and other family members. This important aspect of the baby's development determines whether he will be accepted or rejected by the larger social group. Parents and carers should guide and teach the child to behave in a socially acceptable way, making sure that he understands why the group sometimes disapproves of his behaviour. Although experts believe that by four years of age a child already has a clear understanding of the social group to which he belongs, it may well be much earlier, as even young babies exhibit, through behaviour such as restlessness, an uneasiness in certain circumstances or among certain people. If even a four-day-old baby is clearly more relaxed when people around him speak in his mother tongue, children should also be introduced to, and familiarised with, various other concepts from very early in their lives. This is the first step in the establishment of the child's moral principles.

As children learn best through the example of others, we should behave according to the system that we would like to teach the child. If, according to your value system, lying, swearing, fighting and violence are taboo, that is how you should behave, as your child's value system will develop according to your behaviour and the example that you set. The same goes for the other people in your child's direct environment, so do make sure that other carers and family members comply with your value system. If they do not, your child should not be left alone in their care.

The stronger your own value system is established, and the more visible it is in your life, the more readily your child will adopt your values and learn what is right and wrong, acceptable and unacceptable. On the other hand, doing something today and deciding that it is wrong tomorrow, will confuse your child because your value system is dubious. This leads to more problems regarding discipline, often giving rise to difficult teenage years as well, as the child will still lack a clearly defined value system to follow.

12
Emotions

Although emotional development is just as important as any of the other developmental aspects discussed in the preceding chapters, it is often neglected – not intentionally, but simply because people do not understand it. Some people are prejudiced against anything that looks or sounds like psychology, because they believe that it has to do with 'crazy' people and is far removed from 'normal' people.

However, emotions are an integral part of our lives that determine how we feel, think and react. No part of ourselves stands completely apart from our emotions, each aspect of our day, every task we perform and all our intercourse with other human beings containing an emotional component.

Modern man's obsession with material needs, work satisfaction and success often leads to a dismissal or disregard of our own, and other people's, emotions and emotional needs, not allowing emotion and intuition to interfere with our daily task. Apart from giving rise to higher stress levels, this may also lead to increased levels of frustration, anger and aggression, as well as depression.

To many parents, it is important that their children master all the different tasks at the expected ages, that they are well prepared to perform at school or in a sport, and that they receive the best possible training, sometimes losing sight of the child's own needs. They guide him in everything except listening to his own body's needs, analysing his own emotions and discovering who and what he really is. Parents should teach their children what makes them unique, what makes them special, why they sometimes experience emotions that are hard to cope with, and how to handle emotions that they do not understand.

Our deepest feelings, passions and desires are important guidelines for many of our actions, these deep emotions being greatly responsible for the continued existence of the human race. In life-threatening situations, when there is no time to think, it is our emotions that guide us to make decisions, to act and to survive. Think of the parent who will not hesitate to brave heavy traffic if that could save the life of his child – only undivided love and the pressing emotion to rescue your child from danger can drive a parent to forget about himself and defy danger in order to save his child. Strong emotions have a central place in the human psyche. In times of fear, stress and despair, the heart (emotions) rules over the head (intellect).

Emotions guide us through situations and tasks that are too significant to be entrusted to the intellect alone, such as danger, painful loss, an intimate relationship with a partner, the determination to reach a goal regardless of frustrations, and building a family. Each emotion offers a distinctive readiness to react, implanted in the nervous system as natural inclinations of the human 'heart'. It would be short-sighted to dismiss or disregard emotions. When it comes to decision-making and duty performance, feelings are just as, if not more, important than thoughts.

Intelligence can come to nothing if emotions are not involved. A child's good test results or his achievement on the sports field is indicative of a certain form of intelligence or physical abilities, but gives no indication of the child's emotional development and emotional maturity. The term 'emotional intelligence' is used to describe emotional maturity.

Emotional intelligence

Emotional intelligence involves various abilities, maturing processes and emotional skills, including awakening to, and gaining control over, impulsive behaviour, perseverance, motivation, empathy and social skills. These are the characteristics of people who excel, whose inter-personal relationships flourish and who are the stars in their workplace – the achiever in the classroom or in the workplace usually being the person who is intellectually and emotionally intelligent and mature.

The close relation between emotions and the various sensory systems cannot be over-emphasised. As the sensory systems (see chapter 5) are the most primitive systems in the human body, and emotions can also be regarded as one of the basic systems, both have an important influence on further development and adaptation. Studies have proved that there is a close connection between our sense of touch, in particular, and the limbic system (the brain area for emotions), so that theoretically, a child's maturity can be developed through the integration of the touch system. Emotional maturing has frequently been observed in young children who receive consistent touch therapy for a period of time.[1]

Because our observations, emotions and reactions are always integrated, they can never be separated from one another. When we suddenly come across something that frightens us, for example, a frog, a visual impulse (the sight of the frog) is sent from the retina in the eye to the thalamus in the brain, where it is 'translated' into the language of the brain. From the thalamus, the bulk of this message is sent to the visual cortex, where it is analysed and evaluated to determine the meaning and an appropriate reaction. If the reaction is an emotional one, a message is sent to the amygdala to activate its emotional areas. A smaller portion of the original message goes straight to the amygdala, where a quicker, albeit less accurate, response is evoked. Because the amygdala prompts an emotional response even before the cortical areas are fully aware of what is happening, the person gets a fright even before he is cognitively aware of having seen a frog. In the first milliseconds after we have observed something, we not only unconsciously understand what it is, but also decide whether we like it or not. (Maybe that is why they say first impressions last!)

So it is clear that no action or reaction can stand totally apart from emotions. And as emotions are part of us, we have to teach ourselves and our children to be emotionally intelligent. Not only are emotionally intelligent people excellent workers, but they also know how to effectively deal with the demands of their working day – an unfair boss, difficult colleagues and family problems at home.

Emotional development

Like all other aspects of development, emotional development follows a specific pattern. When a newborn baby experiences emotions, they are expressed through limited behaviours, such as crying. Because the baby has not yet learned different ways of expressing his emotions, however, crying can point to any of a variety of emotions, such as discomfort, anger or sadness. As the baby gets older, he learns to react in different ways.

By around three months, he responds with a little 'social smile' when someone smiles at him. He is also capable of serious, sad or happy facial expressions, usually in conformity with the expressions of the people around him. Later on, he begins to smile at non-social objects, for example at the sight of a familiar or favourite toy. The next step is to express positive emotional reactions, such as smiling when he sees his carers. After that he starts to laugh out loud, enjoying the company of other babies and children. By six months of age, most babies not only enjoy laughing at various simple objects in their environment, but are also capable of crying tears.

The baby increasingly enjoys social contact, albeit mainly physical, for example, kissing, hugging and playfully exploring the bodies of parents and other children. He also becomes more bashful, being apprehensive of strangers and unfamiliar places. At this stage, he probably becomes aware of the existence of a bigger world than his immediate environment, and that his mother sometimes 'disappears' or ceases to be part of the environment. He experiences separation anxiety when he is away from his mother or from another familiar adult. The easy, placid baby who has always been happy to go to anyone, or to sleep anywhere, now suddenly becomes attached to his mother, making it more difficult for her to take him along wherever she goes. He also starts to express anger, which often surprises the parents!

The baby now becomes increasingly experienced in expressing his own emotions, at the same time becoming more attached to, and even possessive over the undivided attention of, his parents or primary carers. His fear of strangers increases rather than subsides, often catching parents unawares as their formerly easy, placid baby becomes more and more demanding.

Fortunately, this stage comes to a close as the child learns more and more about his environment during his first year, his close relationship with his parents and carers giving him the confidence to explore and to discover. His fear of strangers subsides and his curiosity increases.

Closer to the toddler's second birthday, he realises that he is an individual who exists apart from his mother and his carers, also becoming aware of the different roles that he plays in different situations, for example, as a son, a brother and a friend. He now has enough confidence to try and prove his independence and to explore the world – which is exactly where the notorious 'terrible twos' originate from! The one moment he refuses to listen to his mother, often screaming violently to make her understand that he is an independent human being, and the next moment he feels uncertain in this unexplored world, clinging to his mother or carer for security. This is a difficult time for toddler and parents alike! Understanding the reasons for his unsteady behaviour, however, could help the parents to deal with it.

Although the toddler needs security, he also wants to prove himself as an individual, and the parent should give him enough scope to do both. Giving him simple choices to make himself will make him feel in control. For example, let him choose between two or three outfits to wear, or between two different sweets or drinks. Also ask him to help you choose what to wear – if you are going to stay at home, wear the evening dress that he suggests; if not, give him a few outfits to choose from on your behalf.

These simple choices not only give the toddler a measure of authority, but also the security that he is still so badly in need of. Make him feel safe by spending time with him, playing with him, enjoying his company and frequently making physical contact by sitting him on your lap, hugging and kissing him, and playing physical games. Most toddlers enjoy pretending to be a baby again, and being cuddled by the parent as if they were one. This gives them the opportunity to 'escape' from their newly found independence and simply be small again, temporarily reducing the demands they face and giving them the assurance that their emotions, which are often in conflict with one another, are all right.

When a child has successfully gone through this stage, he will have the desire to be independent and self-sufficient, as well as the feeling that he is in control of his own emotions, thoughts and behaviour. This is quite an achievement, especially if you are only three years old!

Social adaptation

The child's basic needs have already been discussed in the chapter on self-image. All children need love, acceptance, success and moderate discipline. Another basic need is companionship with other children of the same age. If the first three needs are met, the child builds confidence in the people around him, while playing with other children gives him the opportunity to acquire social skills, i.e. the ability to hold his own in a social environment through concrete skills such as good manners, but also through various deeper skills that are equally important but not always recognised and expanded. These deeper skills include:

- The ability to confidently communicate with other people.
- The ability to distinguish between necessary and unnecessary guilt. Children sometimes experience unnecessary guilt, for example, when their parents have an argument, while necessary guilt is the guilt that they experience after breaking a rule.
- Acknowledging achievements through approval and encouragement during various activities. Although the child needs to be acknowledged for his own achievements, he must also learn to acknowledge and to value other people's achievements. A toddler is capable of expressing support towards others from a very young age – and meaning what he says.
- The ability to employ the intellect in order to know, understand and discover – thus also the development of curiosity about various environmental aspects. A stimulating environment (see chapter 3) affords the child this opportunity from babyhood.
- The ability to enjoy the aesthetical. As seeing, hearing and touching beautiful things have a particularly calming effect on adults as well as children, visits to different environments should include aesthetic places such as museums, art galleries, scenic parks or gardens, orchestral performances, etc. If they are presented in the right way, the stimulated baby could enjoy and appreciate these environments from a very young age.

- The ability to explore and experience the spiritual aspect of humanity, i.e. an awareness of the reality of God, our Creator. If it is presented in a simple way, the toddler should be able to grasp the concept of divinity. The older toddler could already have a basic knowledge of God who created everything, of people going to heaven and of a divine power that comforts us. These concepts should be explained in a practical, concrete and simple way. Toddlers partially understand these, while preschool children already show an interest in divinity, probably because of the inherent need of every human being to not only understand the world in its concrete form, but also in a spiritual way.

The child's perception of emotions

When you teach your child to control his emotions, and to behave in a socially acceptable way within the directives of his culture, do keep in mind that children and adults express their emotions in substantially different ways. Do not lose heart if you sometimes fail to understand your child's behaviour. Following these guidelines could make your task a little easier:

- Spend plenty of time with your child so that you know what 'wavelength' he is on.
- Know your child well.
- Often make eye contact, getting to know each other's 'eye language'.
- Be alert to other signs of emotion apart from words, in other words, body language. The mere poise of a child's back and shoulders often speaks volumes: despondency, annoyance, irritation, fear.
- Reflect your child's feelings by verbalising the emotion that you observe. Say, for example, "I can see that you are very angry now," then give him the opportunity to agree or to shake his head. Maybe he agrees when you ask something like, "Are you just very hungry?"
- Give your child the opportunity to communicate by showing, or saying how he feels.
- Create a secure environment in which your child feels that he is accepted just the way he is – including all the feelings that he does not even understand himself.
- Talk to your child about your own feelings and emotions (where applicable and always within limits), discussing your own processing of and reaction to these emotions. Say, for example, "I'm not feeling good today, because I am sad that Granny cannot come to visit." This teaches the child that it is okay not to feel good, and that the emotion which he experiences when something that he has been looking forward to does not happen, can be called 'sad'. He also learns that the reason his mom does not laugh and make jokes as usual, is not because he has done something wrong, but because she has her own emotions to deal with.

The following should also be borne in mind:

- Children's emotions are *spontaneous*. As they are still learning, they cannot always exercise self-control, especially when they are younger than two years.
- Children use *defence mechanisms* to deal with their emotions. As the defence mechanism is used to hide the true emotion, there is usually more to the child's reaction than meets the eye. Withdrawal is one example – when a child is shy and does not know how to deal with it, he either withdraws or flees from the situation, sitting on his mother's lap, refusing to play along, running or refusing to make eye contact. The parent should look further than the child's outward reaction, noticing the underlying emotion of shyness. Another defence mechanism is regression, i.e. reverting to a previous development stage. The child may feel guilty because of the tension in his family, losing his ability to use the potty. Instead of regretting the fact that the child is back in nappies, the parent should look for a deeper cause for the child's reaction. Aggression is yet another defence mechanism, typically finding expression in a tantrum and often being nothing more than the child's way of saying that he has no idea what to do with his emotions.
- Children experience things in their own way, which is often different to that of an adult who has a larger frame of reference.

    Arguments between parents often give rise to *guilt* in children. The child could also feel guilty when someone in his family becomes ill or gets hurt, when something in the house breaks, when a loved one passes away or when a parent is seldom home or too busy to explain or verbalise the situation to the child, thinking that it has happened as a result of something that he has done wrong. When something like this happens, the parent should quietly explain to the child exactly what has happened, why it has happened and what the consequences are, or will be. Even if you do not observe any particular emotion in the child as a result of the event, it should still be explained to him, as he probably does not know how to verbalise his questions and guilt. After the event, the parent should continue to regularly talk about what has happened, also giving the child the opportunity to do so, albeit with a limited vocabulary and typical toddler gestures.

    If the child *has* caused a crisis, such as pulling a pot from the stove, the same steps should be followed. The fact that it has happened is probably enough punishment for the child as it is, so do not burden him with any further punishment and guilt. When the cause of the accident is explained to the child, you can tell him that it happened as a result of what he did, but also assure him that you know it was an accident. Explain to him exactly what he has done wrong, asking him never to do it again. Help him think of a way to improve the situation, for example, "Will you help me clean up the mess now?" Also teach him to apologise for his mistake, give him a hug, then leave the matter there. Do not refer to his mistake again.

If you have to repeat it later, be sure to mention that the child has apologised and helped you to clean up, and that it was an accident, not giving the listener the option to judge, punish or make the child feel more guilty.

Although many more emotions can be observed in children, parents should know their children well enough to know *which underlying emotions* are causing their behaviour. Because children have different personalities, the ways in which they observe and react to situations also differ. For that reason, a parent should truly know each of his children. It is interesting to see how differently children from the same family react to the same situation. As this is evident from babyhood, parents can use it as a guideline for getting to know the child's personality and determining in which situations he needs special attention, time and assistance.

Emotions that arise in a child could lead to *high anxiety levels* if the child is left to himself to try and control, quiet an understand those emotions. The parents are the best people to assist the child in this respect.

- Children have a limited ability to *express their feelings in words* – something that even adults struggle with! With his limited vocabulary and frame of reference the child has to try and make sense of the emotions that he experiences. Where possible, parents should try and verbalise the child's feelings, asking him if that is how he really feels. Although we are often wrong, the child is given the opportunity to say yes or no, thereby getting to know his own emotions. For example, when your child is shy in an unfamiliar situation, only wanting to sit on your lap, say something like, "There are so many people here that you don't know and who want to talk to you. Do you want to talk to them?" Your child will probably say no. Then you verbalise his emotion by saying, "You know, sometimes I also feel shy of strangers. But if you sit here with me for a little while just looking at them, they won't look so strange any more. Maybe you will feel like talking to them later." This also teaches him how to handle the situation. In the meantime, allowing your child to sit on you lap will assure him of your unfailing support.

In some situations, however, the child should be encouraged to mix with people, and particularly with other children. Suggest taking his hand and walking with him to the place where the children are playing. Then stay with him for some time, until he lets go of your hand, risking the first steps towards the others alone. Only then can you say to him that you are going back to your seat, assuring him that you will let him know if you are going anywhere – then do not forget to tell him when you are going to the bathroom, for instance, otherwise he may lose his trust in you in this particular situation and you will have to start, trying to get him off you lap all over again. Remember that in an unfamiliar situation, a child does not only feel shy, but is also scared of being left there by himself, so do make sure that he is constantly aware of your whereabouts.

Being a major source of security to the child, the trust relationship between parent and child is something that should be maintained and expanded at all costs. Be honest towards your child at all times, his trust in you being built from the moment that he is born – through your physical care your baby learns that you can be relied on to take good care of him and that you are always there when he needs you.

Knowing your body language better than any other human being, your child (even your young toddler) quickly senses any dishonesty on your part, leading to confusion as to when he can believe you and when not. He starts to feel unsure of the people around him, distrusting others and often doubting your relations or explanations – and you cannot take it amiss!

The first breaching of this trust usually happens when parents slip out, leaving the baby in someone else's care without the child's knowledge. In my mind, this is a major taboo. The child does not know where the parent is, when he is coming back and why he was left behind. No matter if your baby cries when you have to go, say goodbye to him, making sure that he knows that you are leaving. The crying should soon stop when his attention is drawn to something else. A good idea is to leave a personal possession – such as a garment or another personal object – with your baby as a concrete assurance that you will be back again.

Remember, your baby does not understand where you are going; neither does he have any idea when you are coming back or the vocabulary to ask. Being honest with him gives him the assurance that you will never lie to him and that you *will* return as you have promised.

Older toddlers and children quickly sense when parents hold something back from them. When your child asks a question that cannot be answered directly, or when there is a situation in the family or community that cannot, or should not, be discussed with your child, it is better to explain to him that the matter is too sensitive to talk about and that he cannot be told the whole story. Explain to him that there are matters that only grown-ups talk about and that you will explain it to him when the time is right. If you have a trust relationship with your child, he will know that you will never lie to him and that you can be trusted to handle the matter in the best possible way. He will also believe you when you say that it is not in his best interest to hear everything, and that that is the reason why he cannot be told.

This kind of trust relationship between a parent and child could save the parent much distrustfulness, difficult behaviour and bursts of anger – from babyhood through the teenage years and even into adulthood.

---

1. P. Wilbarger and J.L. Wilbarger, *Sensory Defensiveness: A Comprehensive Treatment Approach* (Panorama City, California: Avanti Educational Programs Inc., 2001, revised 2007).

Parenthood

Parents bring their children up in different ways, the method they use determining how the child reacts to various situations within the family and the community, and also how amenable he is to discipline and responsibility, greatly influencing the child's emotional intelligence and social adaptation. For this reason it is of paramount importance that parents should reflect upon the method of education that they choose to follow, in other words, the type of parents that they choose to be, at an early stage.

Parental types

Just as parents have different personalities, so do children. Naturally, this has an effect on the way that you and your child react to, and behave in, different situations. However, a parent can choose a parental type or parental style which he or she would like to follow, irrespective of the parent's or the child's personality. Choosing a parental type is like choosing a sport: Irrespective of your own or the other players' personalities, there are rules that need to be understood and adhered to. During a match, however, your personality and past experiences will probably cause you to behave differently than other team players, still adhering to the rules. Even if you lose your temper completely, you will remember to channel your anger in an acceptable way, or you may lose your place in the team. Similarly, a parent should act according to the rules of the ideal parental type, or the child's emotional intelligence will suffer, making life difficult for parent and child alike. Nobody has time for a child who is emotionally overdependent, rebellious or simply naughty.

There are four basic parental types, which can be summarised as follows:

1. **Dismissive parents** are unconcerned about their child's negative emotions, attaching little importance to his feelings and often saying things like, "Oh, he's still young. I don't pay much attention to his whims." A child with dismissive parents grows up with a poor self-image and low self-esteem, his parents disregarding his intrinsic value, not appreciating and respecting him for the person that he is.
2. **Reproachful or authoritarian parents** are critical when their child shows negative emotions, punishing or rebuking him when he gives expression to his emotions. We often hear them say to the child, "No, it's ugly to cry. You are very naughty now and you are making me unhappy.' "These parents do not allow their children to talk back or to question their authority. Implicit obedience to their commands is regarded as the child's biggest virtue.

    A child who is raised under strict authoritarian control has a whole bunch of psychological problems when he grows up. He becomes neurotic, giving rise to more serious problems, such as eating disorders and depression. Because he never learns to think for himself, make his own decisions or choose the best response in a specific situation, his intelligence and emotional experience become blunted. Whatever his desires, they are never right and never allowed to be fulfilled anyway. In some respects, he becomes a person who acts like a brainless automat or submissive puppet, never becoming a leader and often left to the mercy of any political, religious or business leader who has enough persuasive power.

    Reproachful or authoritarian parents frequently make use of harsh punitive measures. Unfortunately heavy punishment has no positive influence on a child, leading to only one of two outcomes:
    - The fostering of rebellious antagonism in the child, lacking love for the person who administers the punishment; or
    - Identification with the action, the child becoming an aggressive bully just like the parent who administers the punishment.

Heavy punishment further leads to anxiety in children, giving rise to a fear of taking risks in case they do something wrong. As the punishment is seldom in proportion to the infringement, there are many things that these children do not understand. When they grow up, they are often hampered by the fear of being thrashed by a boss or some leader.

Adults who were heavily punished during childhood, struggle to establish firm relationships with people of the same gender as the parent who administered the punishment, giving rise to numerous difficulties, from marital problems to problems with people in authority positions. They often have difficulty dealing with other people's anger as well.

3. *Laissez-faire* **parents** accept their children's emotions and empathize with them, but fail to offer guidance or set limits on their children's behaviour. They typically say, "I feel so sorry for my baby. He was so sad when he could not come along. But what can one do?"

    These parents are often apprehensive of making their own decisions and of transferring their wishes to their children, leaving it to the children to decide and to do as they wish. They are allowed to 'do their own thing', no matter if possessions are damaged or other people get hurt. In actual fact, these parents avoid their parental responsibility by denying their children a structure by which their behaviour can be judged, the tragic being that the children have to learn from bitter experience, such as other people's negative reactions towards them, what is socially acceptable and what is right or wrong.

    Children of laissez-faire parents are prone to anxiety, as they do not know what other people expect from them, what is right or wrong, or how to deal with their own emotions. They feel insecure and are often difficult, unhappy and unpopular.

4. **Emotionally coaching or democratic parents** initially show empathy with their children's emotions, but then proceed to guide them towards dealing with their negative feelings. They coach their children by saying something like, "I can see how sad you are and I'm sorry, but you cannot go with Daddy. Daddy's going to miss you too. You can cry for a little while, but then we are getting some toys with which you can play while Daddy's away. When it is nearly time for Daddy to come home, you can help me make coffee." The child learns that the emotion he experiences is called 'sadness' and that it is okay to feel sad, but that it can be channelled towards a positive outcome (playing with a toy to feel better, caring for someone else).

    These parents set broad limits, offering advice and encouraging their children towards the direction that they regard as the best, also giving them as much freedom to choose as possible. The parents' authority, which is applied wisely, humanely and in the children's best interest, is usually acknowledged by the children. Although children learn to make their own decisions, in the event that a decision has to be forced on a child, the parent supplies reasons for the decision, including an explanation of the alternatives and consequences, encouraging open communication between parent and child.

    This parental style not only yields excellent results as far as emotional development is concerned, but also in the field of intellectual (mental) development. Through this approach alone (paying regard to the child's wishes and ideas whenever possible and encouraging him to make his own decisions) can parents truly influence the direction of their children's lives, ensuring that the values and norms that are important to them will to a great extent be adopted by their children.

Emotional coaching

Looking at the four parental styles, it is quite clear that although the last one, i.e. the emotionally coaching parent, demands the most time when the child is young, it is also the only one that gives him guidance with regard to behaviour, dealing with specific emotions and productive channelling of negative emotions.

As a parent, you may feel unsure about the application of emotional coaching in the numerous situations that you and your child are faced with every day. Keeping the following five steps in mind could simplify your task:

1. Become aware of your child's emotions. And now I repeat what I have been saying throughout the book: Spend time with your child and get to know him – that is the only way that you will become aware of his emotions.
2. Recognise the emotion that you have become aware of as an opportunity to become intimately involved with your child and to teach him.
3. Listen empathically to your child, either to his emotions as perceived in his body language, or if he is old enough to his words.
4. Help the child find the right words to describe his emotion. Say, for example, "I think you are tired," or, "It looks as if you are very angry," or, "Are you sad?"
5. The last step is to set limits and to make suggestions for solving the problem, for example, "It's okay to cry because you feel sad, but only for a short while more," or, "When you are angry, it is okay to hit the punch bag, but not your mom or your brother," or, "Come lie down on the pillow with me, let's take a rest. When one is tired, one feels better after a rest."

Through these five steps the child learns to recognise his emotion. Although it is not always easy to put oneself in the child's position, imagine finding yourself in a completely unfamiliar situation, something that you have never experienced before – then try to verbalise or explain the accompanying emotion. One of the times when a parent experiences unexpected emotions, is probably when the child is left in someone else's care for the first time. One can never be prepared for the flood of emotions caused by dropping off one's child to spend time away from him for the first time in his life. So, think of how you felt (it could also be another unfamiliar experience that you have had), then try to name the feelings and devise a strategy to make it easier for you. Easier said than done, right? Remember, this is how your young child feels when he experiences an emotion – he has no idea what it is, let alone what to do with it. That is why the parent should coach and guide him, making life easier for both of them.

The effects of emotional coaching

Children whose parents constantly provide emotional coaching are far better off than children who do not receive this attention. The effects of emotional coaching are not only visible in the emotional sphere, but ripple out to many other spheres of life. Neither are they left behind with childhood, as the effects remain until deep into adulthood. Although this may sound like hard work and plenty of effort while the child is young, the parent is rewarded with a child who reaches adulthood experiencing relatively few hiccups during his childhood and teenage years.

During the childhood years, a clear difference can be observed between children who are coached emotionally and children who do not enjoy this privilege. Emotionally coached children

- enjoy better physical health
- perform better academically
- get along with friends more easily
- have fewer behaviour problems
- are less involved in violence
- generally experience fewer negative emotions (feelings)
- are generally more positive
- are emotionally healthier
- also experience sadness, anger and fear, but are more capable of comforting themselves in difficult circumstances, being less dependent on others for emotional support
- quickly recover and resume productive tasks after a crisis
- are emotionally more intelligent
- are better protected against the harmful and negative effects of marital problems and divorce.

As you can see, there are various reasons for continual emotional coaching, guiding your child towards emotional maturity. A carer's parental style and ability to provide emotional coaching should be thoroughly investigated before a final decision is made to leave your child in that person's care on a regular basis. The same style and method of coaching that is used at home, should be taken through to the place where you leave your child while you are at work or otherwise occupied.

The father's role

A father who coaches his child emotionally, has a particularly positive impact on the child's emotional development. A child whose father heeds his emotions and feelings, helping him to deal with them, performs better at school as well as in his relationships with other people. In contrast with this, an emotionally absent (or harsh, critical or reproachful) father has an extremely negative impact on the child. Although this does not imply that the mother's influence is inferior, research has shown that the father's influence is more extreme, whether it be positive of negative.

As you may have noticed among family members or friends, people never stop suffering from a poor relationship with their father – even in their old age people are loaded down by the burden of a father who was too harsh, who criticised too much or whose expectations were too high. Whatever the case, if a father does not provide emotional coaching, the child suffers.

I repeat: A parent who spends time with his or her child, who knows the child and who has a close emotional bond with the child, is in a better position to exert influence over the child. When you notice that your child makes a mistake, talk to him about it. Do not be afraid of setting limits. When a parent who is emotionally close to his child tells the child that he is disappointed in him, the child will listen and take the parent's words to heart. The trust relationship between parent and child makes the child receptive to the parent's guidance and advice, easing the parent's task of guiding and motivating the child.

The parent is the best person to provide emotional coaching, knowing which rules he or she wants the child to play to, and being there when his load gets heavy – when he has colic, learns to use the potty, fights with a friend or fails with a task. Your child relies on you for guidance, and it should be given with insight, maturity, empathy and clarity – as could be expected from any good coach.

14

Discipline

The word *discipline* has the same root as *disciple*, which means *someone who learns from somebody else* or *someone who voluntarily follows a leader*. In a family the parents are the leaders and the child the disciple who follows them and learns from them about the ways of life.

Discipline is society's way of teaching a child the moral behaviour that is accepted by the social group in which he lives and grows up. It also prevents him from falling foul of the law when he grows up. The laws of a society are the rules which every group member should live and act by. When these rules are violated, disciplinary measures are taken, which are imperative for the orderly and efficient existence of a society or community.

Discipline teaches a child to assert self-discipline and self-control. Positive disciplining gives rise to an inner motivation that allows continual growth and development of the person until his potential is eventually reached, encouraging and building maturity. Negative disciplining, on the other hand, stunts growth and development, forcing the person to be immature, as it were.

The importance of discipline

Promoting a sense of responsibility, as well as a readiness to obey basic rules and follow a basic routine, discipline is important for the orderliness in any organisation and also in the family. Discipline and routine provide security, a communal spirit and a steadfast basis of values and norms.

Many people regard discipline as a set of rules that must be strictly adhered to and applied in conjunction with punitive measures. Although punishment may suppress certain behaviours, they are not eliminated. Emotional coaching is a much better way of disciplining, teaching the child *why* the behaviour is not allowed. A child who pinches a biscuit, for example, knowing very well that it is not allowed, learns only one thing when he is heavily punished, shouted at or beaten – is that he should be more cautious next time! Emotional coaching teaches the child *why* he may not get a biscuit. Understanding that inwardly motivates him, keeping him from eating too many biscuits later in his life, while punishment only builds up anger, aversion and fear towards his parents.

In order to function properly, every household should have a set of rules to which all members of the family adhere. However, extraneous rules that suppress creativity and independence should be guarded against. Rules should be in everybody's best interest, protecting them against injury or illness, and ensuring that all family members receive recognition, that everyone's possessions are safe, and that they are all given the opportunity to grow and develop.

For example, if a child is allowed to eat as many biscuits as he likes, he will become either fat or sickly later on, as he will not be consuming enough healthy food. In other words, there is a very good reason behind this rule that even a young child can grasp to some extent. To prevent preposterous rules that unnecessarily complicate your own and your child's life, make sure that the rules that you lay down are always justifiable.

A good idea is to have a family meeting where rules are laid down and explained, together with applicable 'punitive measures'. Allowing the child to be part of the decision-making process helps to build self-image, independence and inner motivation. Keep it very simple and concrete while the child is still young, allowing him to become more involved as he gets older – also on an abstract level later on.

As we have seen, moderate control or discipline is a basic need in every child, being indispendable for the following reasons:

1. It gives the child a strong feeling of security.
2. It eliminates frequent feelings of guilt and shame caused by bad behaviour.
3. It enables the child to behave according to the accepted standards of the social group to which he belongs.
4. It teaches the child to behave in a way that evokes frequent praise, which is experienced as love and acceptance.

5. If correctly applied, it builds a child's self-image, motivating him to do what is expected of him.
6. It helps the child to develop a conscience, enabling him to make his own decisions and control his behaviour.

From the very first months of a child's life, parents should be consistent with regard to what is right and what is wrong. A child who grows up with definite rules and a clear understanding of right and wrong from a very young age, handles discipline, advice and admonitions far better when he is older. Rules and admonitions should be emotionally coaching, however, aimed at building the child, improving his understanding and helping him to adjust more easily, and not at belittling or frightening the child.

Punishment

A young child needs to know and understand the rules before he can intentionally break them. He cannot be punished for a violation if the parent is not convinced that he knows and understands the relevant rule. He somehow needs to learn the difference between right and wrong, however – therefore it is acceptable to apply moderate punishment, such as raising your voice when the child does something that could be harmful to himself or to others. After all, a child cannot be allowed to play with a sharp knife just because he does not know that it is wrong yet. In this case the punishment will be to remove the knife. As soon as the child is old enough to understand the meaning of words, language should be used to replace the punishment.

As we have seen in the chapter on parenthood, a child who receives undue punishment can develop various problems (see Reproachful or authoritarian parents, page 133). The following are some vital elements contained in constructive punishment:

1. The punishment should be in proportion to the transgression and administered as soon as possible after the misbehaviour, enabling the child to lay a link between the two.
2. The punishment should be consistent, teaching the child that when a rule is violated, punishment inevitably follows. This way the child will not 'take chances' to see what happens or how the parent reacts. While inconsistent reactions by the parent could turn into an interesting game for the child, consistent discipline puts an end to the behaviour as the child knows exactly what the consequences will be.
3. Whichever method of punishment is used, it should never be personal. Punish the deed without falling into nastiness or belittling the child.
4. The punishment should be constructive, guiding and motivating the child to behave socially acceptably in the future.

5. Explaining the reason for the punishment will help the child to experience it as fair.
6. Punishment should help the child to develop a conscience, enabling him to apply self-control.
7. Punishment should never humiliate the child.

A democratic parent, whose child is coached emotionally, should experience few disciplinary problems, as the child will believe in himself and understand why certain deeds, behaviours and activities are impermissible. All parents' patience is tried at some stage, however, often giving rise to uncertainty as to how to act in the best interest of the child's emotional development. This is perfectly normal, as there is no way that every situation that you and your child will ever find yourselves in, can be foreseen and described in a book. Keeping in mind the five steps of emotional coaching, and the seven ingredients of constructive punishment, should help you cope with most of your situations, as a positive self-image in the child, and good communication within the family, make disciplining a child much easier.

As mentioned earlier, children frequently test their parents to see how far they can go. For a parent this can be emotionally exhausting. Imagine the parents as a house, with the child standing inside the house, testing the strength of its walls by pushing, kicking, hitting or pounding against them. If the walls remain steady, the child feels safe and inwardly secure. However, if the walls collapse like those of a flimsy tent, or frequently react in different ways every time that they are tested, the child feels scared and unsafe, experiencing anxiety instead of security. In an attempt to find security, the child continues to push, kick, hit and pound against the walls. When discipline and punishment are applied consistently, and when the same punitive measures are consistently used for the same transgression, the child feels safe and secure with the parent.

Routine

Young children generally react positively to a routine and to consistent discipline. A home and family routine provides the child with a feeling of security, allowing him to know exactly where he stands with a parent and what can be expected next, for example, after bath time it is supper time, followed by story time and then sleep time. A child who is in a routine feels safe, knowing what is expected of him and experiencing enough security to allow him to risk and explore, keeping himself 'occupied' for fair amounts of time.

No family can be expected to stick to a specific routine at *all* times. However, there is a big difference between a temporary interruption in your routine and having no routine at all. When the routine is interrupted, the child still has the security of something safe and familiar, allowing him to make adjustments with this framework as reference. If there is no routine, the child has no system to hold onto and to measure himself by, making him feel unsure of what is expected of him, how to behave, and how to react in the particular circumstances.

When the routine is interrupted, it is a good idea to prepare the child for the change as soon as he is old enough to understand. For example, when your evening routine is to be interrupted because you are receiving guests, you will make life easier for both of you by preparing your young child for the situation. Explain to him that you are expecting visitors and that you would like him to bath and eat earlier, for instance. After supper he will be allowed to sit with you for a while, but you will not have time to read him a story. Also explain to him how you would like him to behave, for example, greet the people, not play with his noisy toys or watch TV, but that you will allow him to sit on your lap and play with a special toy or book. If, after explaining to the child what will be expected of him, the parent also makes sure that he behaves in that way, it will soon become a habit and the parent will find that the child is particularly well behaved in the company of visitors, just as he has been taught.

If, however, rules are laid down beforehand but the parents fail to see them through, the child learns that it is unnecessary to obey, as it is not expected of him to do as he was told anyway. This child will probably be extremely difficult, the parents having only themselves to blame as they are the ones who taught the child to disobey in the first place! Besides, the child will not know how to behave, trying every possible way to test the parents' reaction, who will end up spending very little time with their guests as they will be running after their 'disobedient' child all evening. This not only leads to an unsatisfactory time in the company of the guests, but also to negative reactions to the child's behaviour that are destructive to his self-image. If the parents do not teach the child how to behave in certain situations, he will continue to try all sorts of behaviour, driving the parents to desperation.

Obedience

As explained above, emotional coaching and routine are vital if a parent is to get the child's cooperation. This cooperation is what we call 'obedience'. Obedience does not imply that the child slavishly obeys orders in fear of punishment when failing to do so, but rather that he understands the rules, requests and commands, as well as the reasons behind them, reacting to them of his own free will. Inner motivation and self-control are what drive the child to act in accordance with the expectations of the parent and the group.

A child who has a trust relationship with his parents and who receives emotional coaching, generally cooperates well. Even when a situation arises that he does not understand, he trusts the parents, listening to them and obeying their commands.

Of course children will test their parents – not only their patience, but also their willingness to follow through on what they said. Remember that this gives the child security.

When he tries to oppose you, he is actually just testing the walls of his house to make sure that he lives in a solid house that constantly remains the same. It also gives him the assurance that your rule is genuine, that his actions are noticed, that his behaviour matters to you and that you always act the same. There are few things as confusing to a child as a parent who reacts inconsistently.

Parents often fall into the habit of saying *no*, rather than trying to use the word as sparingly as possible. Hearing *no* too often can be destructive to a child's self-image. If *no* is limited to essential use only, such as disciplining a child, its impact will be greater and the child will know that the parent is serious. For example, when your child asks if something is blue, your answer should be, "It is green" rather than, "No, it's green."

So, to teach a child obedience *no* should only be used when the child is actually doing something that is not allowed. The parent should then make sure that the child reacts immediately. Parents often complain that they have to say *no* repeatedly before their toddler will listen – the reason being that the parent has taught him so! Reacting promptly by removing either the child or the object after you have said *no*, teaches the child to listen immediately, and it soon becomes a habit.

Honesty

To ensure that he gets the child's cooperation, the parent has to keep his part of the agreement as well, being open and honest with the child at all times. When the parent tells a lie or a half-truth, the child is sure to detect it – and to start doing as he has learnt through example! Have you ever watched a toddler imitate his parents? He can faultlessly repeat their tone of voice, their body language and even their words. That is evidence of how closely he can perceive, how narrowly he watches his parents, how well he knows them and how much he learns from them. A parent should never say, "My child won't notice." He is highly likely to notice, and by ignoring it the parent misses an opportunity to teach the child. Rather be honest, even if you have acted wrongly or made a mistake – that is part of life, and some or other time the child has to learn that his parents are not perfect and that they, too, make mistakes, like all other human beings.

By being honest himself, the parent also conveys this quality to his child, who will not only be honest with respect to obeying rules and laws, but also in his relationship with other people, his relationship with friends and, most importantly, his relationship with himself. Honesty towards oneself is the first step towards self-knowledge and self-acceptance, notwithstanding all one's good and bad qualities, talents and shortcomings. This is something that many adults lack, with sad consequences for the person himself, as well as for those close to him. Parents should seize the opportunity to encourage honesty in their child from a very young age.

15
Problem solving and conflict

Solving problems

Problem solving is part of our everyday lives, often taking up the biggest portion of our day. Effective problem solving involves 'thinking of something' that could improve our immediate circumstances. Children, as well as adults, frequently struggle with solving their own problems, giving rise to either short-term unhappiness or long-term depression, and sometimes encouraging negative behaviour, such as addictions or unsocial behaviour like crime.

Although an inability to solve problems is often the result of a poor self-image, it can more often be blamed on a lack of experience. A good self-image provides a person with the confidence to seek excellent advice in order to overcome his problem, while someone with a poor self-image is often too shy or too unsure to ask for help. (Thinking of your own school days will probably yield examples of both these types.)

Children who have been overprotected by their parents often find it difficult to learn a new skill or to solve a problem, their natural urge to explore and to experiment having been suppressed by parents who have made decisions and solved problems on their behalf. Never having learned to rely on their own abilities, their parents always having decided for them what is safe and right, these children frequently prefer to leave problem solving to their parents or to another willing person.

Parents who have confidence in their child's ability to solve his own problems, accepting and praising the method that the child has chosen (even if the parent would have used another method himself), encourage the child to be adventurous without taking unnecessary risks. This child tackles new tasks and problems with confidence, asking for help and advice where necessary, and experimenting with creative ways of performing tasks and solving problems later on.

The following are some ways in which problem solving can be encouraged in babies and toddlers:

- Stimulate and develop a good self-image in your child.
- Show your child, from his baby days to his teen years and beyond, that you have confidence in his abilities.
- Give your child the opportunity to make his own decisions, making him feel that he is in control and that his opinion counts. As we have seen in the chapter on self-image, these decisions should be simple and within the child's ability. Because the child does not have enough knowledge and experience to actually make decisions yet, he should be given two or three options to choose from – just make sure that these are concrete and within his frame of reference. While the child cannot be expected to decide where he wants to live, for example, he can decide what he wants to wear, which game he would like to play, which story you should read to him, even which friend he would like to invite over. The child should also be taught to accept the consequences of, or take the responsibilty for, his decisions, developing in him the ability to think and to plan ahead – important aspects of adult life.
- Use the numerous opportunities offered by games and your daily family life to teach your toddler how to solve problems. Here are some examples:
  » Spilling juice (first wipe the table to prevent more juice from dripping onto the floor, wash the floor to remove the stickiness, rinse the cloth afterwards, drink some from the cup so that it is not so full)
  » Reaching for something outside his reach (too high – stand on a chair; too far – use another object to bring it closer)
  » Building a simple jigsaw puzzle
  » Clambering over and under an obstacle course built with furniture, blankets and toys
  » A friend getting hurt (comfort, fetch a plaster)
- Always praise your child's efforts to solve a problem. A creative child will probably come up with impossible solutions, which can be extremely valuable in numerous aspects of his adult life. Never say, "No, that won't work," or burst into laughter, as such a reaction inhibits the child, causing him to rely on your guidance the next time instead of thinking up his own plan again. Rather say something positive, such as, "Yes, that sounds like a good idea. Maybe we should think of more." Discuss the consequences of the different solutions, then help him choose the best one. If the

child comes up with a good solution, it should be applied immediately so that he can see that his plan works. This serves to build the child's self-image, encouraging him to plan independently the next time.

A child learns responsibility when he sees the result of his decision or action. However, this does not mean that a parent should allow everything that the child chooses to do just so that he can learn by his own actions – that would be laissez-faire parenting. The responsible, emotionally coaching parent guides the child, teaching him the consequences of his actions. Positive as well as negative consequences should be pointed out. Although parents are inclined to focus on the negative aspects, toddlers sometimes come up with the niftiest positive-outcome plans. When your two-year-old attempts to clean up after making a mess, for example, praise him for having made a good decision, pointing out the consequences of his decision as well: the floor is clean, Mommy is happy and he gets a hug!

Although your child cannot understand abstract ideas during his baby and toddler years, he can no doubt understand concrete cause and effect. A parent should seize every possible opportunity to teach a child that everything we do always has an effect. As his concept of time is still largely undeveloped, there have to be immediate concrete results. In the example of the toddler cleaning the floor, the clean floor and the parent's hug are concrete effects, while the emotion of happiness is also conveyed by the word 'happy', together with the mother's friendly face and approval of his deed.

Dealing with conflict

If your toddler's action has a negative effect (refusal to obey you, for example), immediate reaction is required. Remove him from whatever it is that he is doing, punish him in an appropriate way, explain the consequence and settle the matter there and then. Remaining angry for a long time afterwards will upset both you and your child, and the child will not understand what it is about.

Always react in a positive, concrete manner when your baby or toddler obeys you, keeps himself busy, behaves in a socially acceptable way and performs or attempts to perform tasks in the house. Through your positive reaction the child learns that good behaviour has positive effects, encouraging him to behave in this way more frequently in order to experience more of the parent's positive reactions. Positive feedback also assures the child of your acceptance and your confidence in his abilities, giving him the confidence to accept responsibility.

All families have days when it feels as if everything is going wrong. Often when the parent's energy levels are low, that is also the time when the baby or toddler is particularly difficult and demanding. If the parent has frequently reacted negatively towards the child during the day, a special attempt should be made to balance that out with positive reactions before bedtime. Sometimes it is necessary to pick the child up and tell him how much you love him; sometimes you can make sure that he takes part in activities which he can be praised for (for example, 'help' to prepare supper or play quietly in the bath), and other times you can read him a special story or sing a song with him. Often, on such a difficult day, the baby or toddler simply gets too few positive reactions from the parent or sees too little of him or her. He is not really difficult; he is just asking for your undivided attention. Before the day is over your child should be assured that everything is okay, even though it has been a tough day. Then you can both sleep peacefully, in the assurance that the next day should be a 'normal' day again.

Conclusion

Although we have reached the end of the book, your path with your child definitely does not end here! It is my hope that you have been inspired to find out more, to spend more time with your child, to be alert to him and to escort and guide him on his way to adulthood. Although the first three years of a child's life are of the utmost importance, plenty more time and energy should be spent on 'coaching', educating and stimulating your child in the years to follow. Nobody will have a bigger influence on your child than his parents, his primary carers.

Accompanying your child on his way to adulthood – sharing in his life and experiencing his heartaches, excitements, glories and expectations with him – is a wonderful adventure. It is a privilege to see how your child develops, how his personality unfolds and how he becomes a person in his own right. Just like no two human beings are the same, no two children of a family can ever be the same. So, enjoy discovering and experiencing your child's unique potential, personality, taste, abilities *and* inabilities with him as he grows up.

Never stop reading, watching, listening and learning, as these will help you to become an informed parent, enabling you to be the best possible coach that your team – your own family – can have.

Appendix 1

A stimulating environment in practice

Newborn babies

During the first weeks after his birth, the baby is still getting used to his new environment. Although some stimulation is needed, it should be limited to a minimum, as overstimulation leads to tenseness and restlessness. A young baby not only needs enough time to sleep in peace and silence, but also to lie awake by himself, getting familiar with his environment.

If a baby is restless without any apparent physical reason, it could be a symptom of overstimulation and the baby should be allowed more time to process new information. This is often the case when the parents receive frequent visitors or when the baby is taken along on a family outing. In both circumstances the parents are often quite busy, getting tired and not noticing how many different people handle the baby, talk to him or try to feed him. There is also much more noise in the form of voices and/or music – all of which are unfamiliar experiences, leading to an increase in the baby's stress levels. Removing your baby from the busy environment to a place where he feels more secure will allow him to digest the sensory 'overload'.

From the fifth month of pregnancy, your baby will enjoy listening to **classical music**. Playing the same music in the first months after his birth that he has listened to during your pregnancy will help to relax your baby.

Talk and **sing** often in your baby's presence. The more language he is exposed to, the more his language ability will be stimulated and the better it will develop.

During the first weeks after his birth, the baby's visual cortex is particularly active. His **mother's face** is one of the very first objects that he recognises. Frequently hold your baby in such a way that he can look at you face – for example, while you are breastfeeding. Even a bottle-fed baby can be held in this position (touch stimulation), enabling him to hear his mother's voice (auditory stimulation) and to see her face (visual stimulation). Few things are as fulfilling for a mother as to see her baby studying her face and making eye contact with her! The father should do the same, enabling the baby to get to know his dad's face as well.

During the last few weeks of pregnancy, there is limited space in the womb for free movement of the baby, which results in him feeling fairly insecure in his new, spacious environment shortly after birth. For that reason, your baby should be **tightly wrapped** in **blankets** during the first two weeks or so. When, after this period, he starts to show more movement, it is an indication that he no longer wants to be so tightly wrapped.

Touch stimulation is vitally important for optimal development in a baby. Here are some methods that will promote stimulation in your young or newborn baby:

- Massage your baby before and after bath time, rubbing his body with **oil** all over (olive or almond oil is relatively cheap). Start by rubbing very gently, using firmer movements as the baby gets older.
- Use a **soft towel** to dry your baby, keeping in mind that his skin is still very soft and tender.
- Use soft **clothes** and **blankets**.
- As your baby gets older, other **textures** such as a sponge, brush and cream or oil can be used.

During the first few weeks, the vestibular sense (sense of movement) can be stimulated by **handling** your baby. Being picked up, fed, changed, winded and carried around will give the baby plenty of movement stimulation, while slow rocking movements will calm a restless baby.

The **mother's smell**, as well as other, unfamiliar smells in the baby's environment, provides enough stimulation for the young baby's sense of smell. Likewise, the taste of breast milk, and probably also of water, offers enough stimulation for his sense of taste.

Young babies who have yet to master sitting up

At this stage, the visual cortex, which is active from directly after the baby's birth, develops rapidly. The baby, who now stays awake for longer periods of time, is also more alert to objects in his environment, being able to follow a person around the room with his eyes.

Place **pictures** inside your baby's cot to look at when he is awake, making sure that they are in his field of vision. If you hang something above his bed, looking at it from your baby's vantage point will give you an idea whether it will provide enough stimulation for the baby. If the baby's cot is used for sleep only, show the baby the pictures when he is not in the cot, or place them in the cot when he is not sleeping.

You may find that certain pictures will calm your baby. Use these to calm him before he goes to sleep, or if he needs to sleep while on an outing away from his familiar environment. Black and white, as well as shades of grey, can be perceived from a very young age. Although there is no consensus as to when a baby starts to identify colours, he does focus on strongly contrasting colours – such as black and white – for longer periods of time. Tie cards with simple patterns or pictures in strongly contrasting colours to the inside your baby's cot. Do not suffice with black and white – red on white, and blue on white, or dark green on light yellow is just as effective (and the same cards can be used to teach him the colours later on!). Making a few sets will allow you to alternate them daily.

When your baby is a little older, **different pictures or objects** can be hung above his bed. Although expensive toys from a toy shop may look pretty, a cheap, **home-made** option works just as well and can be alternated more regularly. Six butterflies above his bed will not stimulate or enrich your baby for very long!

Holding a **brightly coloured object** in your hand, slowly move it in all different directions (forward, backward, left, right, diagonally and in a circle), encouraging your baby to follow it with his eyes. Apart from strengthening the eye muscles that control the eyeball, this also teaches the baby to focus at different distances.

Once the baby starts to move his arms and legs more actively, he learns that there is a reason for moving his limbs, in other words, that his limbs have a function. The first time that this happens is when he accidentally bumps against something, causing a reaction. Hang a **toy low enough above his bed** so that when he moves his hands, they will bump against the toy. There are beautiful, colourful toys available in every price range, or you can make your own by threading various shapes onto a string and hanging them above your baby's bed (painted papier-mâché shapes are very effective). Attaching colourful objects to a sturdy string, using clothes pegs or file clips is also a good idea if objects are to be alternated. The advantage of homemade objects is that they are cheaper, giving you a bigger variety for your money. Alternate them regularly, keeping in mind that your baby needs time to practise – once he manages to bump against the toy, causing a reaction, he should be allowed to 'practise' with the same toy for a few days until he can do it more easily and more voluntarily. When he starts losing interest, it should be replaced, offering him a new challenge.

Using **different textures** during bath and dressing time gradually introduces your baby to a bigger spectrum of touch sensations. Make a blanket using differently textured fabrics on which your naked baby can roll before or after his bath. At this stage, bath time should be a delightful experience for both you and your baby. Making eye contact, cuddling and playing with your baby, naming his body parts as you wash and dress him, and singing songs, all add to a particularly pleasant time of togetherness.

The baby uses his **mouth**, which contains numerous nerve ends or receptors, to explore his environment. Instead of removing everything from his mouth, the baby should be given a wide variety of objects of different shapes and textures to put into his mouth. Wash these objects regularly and do not allow more than one baby to use the same objects, unless they are cleaned in between. Keep a basin with a weak antiseptic solution ready in your kitchen in which objects can be dunked directly after use. Washing them once a day will ensure that your baby always has something interesting to investigate. These objects may be toys as well as everyday household items like plastic bowls, plastic spoons, pots and pans, plastic bathroom containers, and even clothes, old magazines and books – as long as they are clean and contain no parts that can hurt the baby, come undone or come open. Be especially mindful of small parts that can choke your baby.

By now the baby has become used to the different sounds outside the womb, through his mother's voice remains the most familiar and most comforting sound to him. Keep on **singing** and **talking** to your baby, encouraging the father to do the same. Regularly play **classical music** in the nursery as well as in the rest of the house. By hearing nursery songs and rhymes, your baby also gets to know the rhythms and sounds, even though he cannot react to them yet.

Begin to introduce your baby to more **smells and tastes** now, even if he does not eat solids yet. Allow him to smell different fragrances, such as your perfume. Seal soft toys in plastic bags together with different herbs – after a day or so, when the toy has adopted the subtle herb flavour, the toy can be placed near your baby or given to him to play with. Aromatherapeutic oils are too strong and should be avoided, as they may lead to negative reactions in babies. If your baby finds a certain flavour unpleasant, it can be removed – there is no reason why he should get used to something that he does not like.

Vestibular stimulation still takes place when your baby is cared for, picked up and carried around. A pouch or papoose will help you carry your baby with ease, while he also experiences your body smell and sounds, giving him a feeling of security. Gently **rocking** your baby while holding him in your arms, either in the stomach or in the back position, pacifies him, while faster movements lead to higher levels of activity and alertness. At this stage, the parents can lay the baby down on a towel or small blanket, gently rocking him from side to side while tightly holding the four corners. Guard against playing too roughly shortly after supper or before bedtime, as this may lead to nausea or overexcitement which could keep your baby awake.

Slow, deep touching or stroking, and slow rocking movements pacify a restless baby before sleep time. This should not be done too often, however, as it can become a problem when your baby refuses to go to sleep without them, especially when he starts getting heavier. Only use them when playing with your baby or when there is a reason for his restlessness, such as an unfamiliar environment or a routine that is temporarily interrupted.

The baby now becomes more active, starting to **squirm and roll over**. This should be encouraged by regularly laying the baby down on a mat, placing different toys or interesting objects nearby. Reaching for them encourages movement, which in turn promotes motor development. By alternating the stomach and back positions different muscle groups are exercised. You can also begin to play some of the games described under Vestibular senses in chapter 5 (see page 55).

With the baby lying in the back position, leg movements can be encouraged by holding an object near his feet that makes a noise when being kicked against (a tinfoil pie plate is ideal!). The baby now starts grabbing objects and, as we have already seen, he can seize (and clutch!) before he can let go. The more different objects he is given to handle and to investigate, the better, as this also gives him the opportunity to practise the letting go action. With the finer coordination of the hands and fingers now starting to develop, the baby becomes interested in picking up **smaller objects**. A set of measuring spoons makes a good toy, as it is easy to hold and to shake.

Attractive and useful **baby seats** are available on the market that allow babies to sit in a comfortable position, and can also be used for transporting a baby. The baby should not be left in the seat for long periods, however – remove him from the seat as soon as your destination is reached, laying him down on a mat instead to encourage movement. When your baby is not asleep or in your arms, he should always be laid down on the floor or on a similar surface, where his movements will not be restricted.

This is also the stage when babies start to enjoy **hiding games**. Hold a cloth in front of your face, then take it away saying, "Peek-a-boo! I see you!" Through this game, the baby learns that although the parent is sometimes not visible, he or she still exists.

The baby remains interested in the many faces that he gets to know. You can now start to look through **books and photo albums** with your baby, pointing out people and animals. He also enjoys seeing himself in **a mirror**. Laying you baby down in the stomach position in front of a mirror motivates him to lift up his head, strengthening his neck muscles and preparing him for sitting and crawling.

Babies who can sit on their own, but have yet to master crawling

At this stage, the baby is more independent, having his arms free to investigate and play with objects. His manual dexterity now needs to be exercised, and his torso muscles strengthened, in order to prepare him for crawling.

As the visual and motor components now start working together, the baby does not touch objects incidentally any longer, but looks at a specific object, reaching to pick it up. Hand-eye coordination develops rapidly and should be stimulated, using the following toys:

- **Soap bubbles.** A series of tiny soap bubbles is visually attractive and encourages the baby to try and touch them, while some of the larger ones could land on a soft surface, giving him the opportunity to actually 'catch' one.
- **A fair-sized ball.** Move a ball (approximately 20 cm in diameter) from side to side in front of the baby, encouraging him to try and catch or kick the ball. His eyes will also follow the ball.
- **A jack-in-the-box.** An animated toy such as a jack-in-the-box not only keeps the baby occupied visually, but also encourages him to reach for the toy, trying to touch it.
- **Old magazines.** An old magazine or colourful newsprint not only provides visual impulses, but also motor and auditory impulses when it is handled and torn.
- **Balls of different sizes.** Provide your baby with balls which can be held, rolled and thrown. Apart from his hand-eye coordination, his perception of distance is also developed as the balls move closer to and further away from him.

With bilateral integration also developing now, the two sides of the baby's body start to collaborate. He can handle objects with both hands, holding his bottle by himself and also starting to **clap his hands**. Toys than can be shaken, such as plastic containers filled with dry pasta, rice or sand, are not only visually attractive, but if the containers are big enough, the baby will also be forced to use both hands, promoting bilateral integration. **Musical instruments** or **pots, pans and wooden spoons** are ideal for the stimulation of rhythm and bilateral integration.

Perceptual concepts such as inside/outside and above/below start to develop. Fill containers with **smallish objects** that the baby can throw out and put back in. Name colours and shapes, and say the names of objects and toys, continuing to talk to you baby as often as possible.

With his fine coordination developing further, the handling and manipulation of small objects become easier by the day. An **activity board** inside the baby's cot or on the mat provides excellent stimulation.

Bath time is a delightful opportunity for your baby to play and to spend time with his parents. Provide him with a variety of toys, making sure that there are different textures and colours, as well as something that can float, sink and pour water. Use differently fragranced soaps. Bath foam provides another touch sensation, as do the different sponges and cloths that you use for washing your baby. Name the child's body parts (also your own, especially if you are with him in the bathtub) and say the names of his toys. This playtime and special time spent with the parent should form part of the child's bath-time routine until he is much older, even just before he goes to formal school!

The baby now increasingly enjoys games that stimulate the different senses, at the same time serving as preparation for crawling.

Crawling babies who have yet to master walking

When the baby starts to crawl, the parent and baby are usually equally relieved, as this brings and end to the baby's frustrations regarding his dependency with respect to movement. This relief is short-lived, however, as a baby can disappear out of sight in a flash, enjoying his newly found independence – at the cost of the parents who have to watch him 24/7!

The baby now practises and expands the hand-eye coordination, bilateral integration and motor skills that he acquired in the previous stage. Visual and auditory perception also develop fast, and toys that should be at the baby's disposal include the following:

- A cupboard containing toys and objects such as **plastic bowls** which the baby can unpack and investigate, match and fit together, and which will help him make discoveries, e.g. some make a noise when they are shaken, some are soft and others have a fragrance. If the contents are updated regularly by replacing some of the objects and adding new ones, your baby will love playing and exploring there, leaving you with a couple of hours to yourself every day!

- A pit or container with **clean sand** where the baby can play and bury objects. Sand provides good touch stimulation, while the scooping and pouring of sand, as well as objects that are 'lost' and found again, aid perceptual development. The sand should be sterile at all times.
- Some **cushions and blankets** to crawl under and over, and to fall and play on.
- Toys that require a **motor action** to cause a reaction, such as a knob that has to be pressed or turned to make something open up or jump out.
- **Large wooden blocks** that gradually help the baby to master concepts such as **above, below, in front, behind** and **next to**. Babies learn to build a **train** (horizontal line) before they can master a **tower** (vertical line).
- Simple **one-piece wooden jigsaw puzzles** with a knob for easy handling, or a large **shape-sorter** with easily manipulable parts. The baby can now start to fit shapes into openings. Although he may still need lots of assistance, the concept will be established.
- **Stacking toys** such as containers that are stacked or fitted together from big to small. These can be used in various ways to teach a baby the concepts of 'large' and 'small'.
- A **pet** such as a rabbit, goldfish or bird to teach the baby the basic concepts of caring. As he starts to enjoy nature now, your baby will love crawling around on the **lawn** and playing with (or among) **dry leaves**.
- Continue to use **musical instruments, songs, language, books** (for reading to the baby as well as for handling himself) and **classical music**.

The baby now enjoys throwing his toys on the floor from where he is sitting in his high chair or on a parent's lap. Although the parent may become bored and tired of picking up toys, which are promptly thrown to the floor again, the baby learns about cause and effect, at the same time developing his perception of distance. By throwing objects and seeing how they become smaller as they fall, he learns that when an object appears smaller, it is probably further away from him. As the learning process requires repetition, the parent will simply have to be patient and keep bending down time after time!

The more a baby crawls, the better, so do not encourage walking by doing special exercises with your baby. Neither should a walking ring be used. Once the baby has mastered crawling well enough, he will start pulling himself up against furniture and pushing large objects – such as a laundry basket – around the house, strengthening his legs and improving his balance. Before you know it, he will be walking like a pro.

Walking toddlers

Initially still practising his balance, the toddler should be allowed to walk and run around as much as possible. As he gets stronger, he risks more, walks further and starts to clamber. These motor actions not only strengthen his muscles, but also teach him various perceptual concepts, further improving his balance in order to adapt to his growing body and his head getting further away from the ground. The games described in the chapter on sensory development can now be applied with great success. Besides the toys already mentioned in this appendix, your child will also benefit from the following:

- climbing and clambering equipment, a slide, a scooter and later on a tricycle
- balls of different sizes and weights
- jigsaw puzzles to match his ability
- paint, crayons, finger paint, paper and play dough
- toy cars of different sizes
- soft toys and dolls with blankets and clothes
- buckets of different sizes with lids (and/or your plasticware cupboard)
- wooden blocks
- shape-sorters and containers to hold shapes
- books, for reading to your baby as well as for handling himself
- music to listen to, sing along with and dance to (classical and children's music)
- musical instruments (and/or your pots, pans and wooden spoons)
- household items such as a toy broom, pots, cutlery, etc.
- a toy workbench with tools
- a mirror at a height where he can see his own image
- a swing to match his ability
- a pet or garden that needs nurturing
- opportunities to share with and share out to others and to take care of them in some way (although 'sharing' is still a difficult concept for the toddler)

A home conducive to stimulation

As there will be children in your home for at least some years to come, it should be equipped to accommodate their needs. However, this does not mean that your house has to resemble a nursery school. Although some houses may be big enough to have a separate nursery and playroom, others could be too small. Be that as it may, there should be enough space left for the parents to also enjoy **their** special times, to receive their friends and to continue living a 'normal' life even though they are full-time parents now. Children should be taught from a young age that certain places are to be respected and that they cannot always do what they wish, wherever they want.

A child-friendly house does not imply an untidy house – it is merely a house where children feel at home and where grown-ups can relax because it is a safe environment for their children. There should be a special room or corner for your baby and his toys. Although the child will need more space as he gets older, it can still be restricted to a kitchen cupboard, a corner in the lounge and a corner in your bedroom, for example. If a child is taught from a young age that those are his spaces, that that is where his toys and clothes are kept and that that is where he can play undisturbed, he will understand and abide by your arrangement.

The following are the minimum spaces that your baby will need until he reaches toddlerhood:

- his own bed in his own room or a corner of your room
- his own cupboard in which his clothes are kept
- a cupboard for his toys (Place this cupboard near a mat on which the baby can play, adding a small table and chair later on. A child who always has toys available to play with, learns to keep himself busy – toddlers love play dough, crayons and blackboards. If the child can go to the play area by himself, use his own initiative and keep himself occupied, both parent and child will have more space for themselves.)
- colourful pictures and objects around the play area
- soft, subdued colours and silence, or classical music, around his sleeping area
- a quiet corner to retreat to (A large beanbag or his bed should be sufficient. Alternatively, buy a small tent and furnish it with soft cushions in subdued colours. When your toddler feels sad, peakish or simply overstimulated, he can retreat to this place to 'realign' himself sensorically. Some books and music could add to its value.)

A safe environment

- When hanging something up, great care should be taken to ensure that it will not come loose when the baby pulls on it – he could be stronger than you think. Because a baby can seize before he can let go, he often clutches, pulls and tugs unintentionally!
- Toys and toy components should always be big enough not to be swallowed by a baby.
- Wash toys regularly, as they often find their way to a baby's mouth.
- Using toys and other objects of an excellent quality prevents not only injuries, but also unhappiness when a favourite object or toy becomes unusable.
- Read books and pamphlets on safety in and around the house, following their advice to create a safe environment for your child. All too often we hear and read about children who got drowned, burnt or crippled. As these are accidents that can be prevented, we should do everything in our power to ensure that our own families do not become part of the statistics.

Appendix 2 - Recipes

Papier-mâché

There are three recipes that work equally well.

Recipe 1
Cake flour, water and paper (old newsprint works well, as the glue will be easily absorbed). Using three parts water and one part flour, mix to a creamy consistency. A few drops of oil can be added to extend shelf life (wintergreen oil is available from most pharmacies). Mix well, dip torn paper strips in the mixture, then layer them onto the shape to be covered.

Recipe 2
Wallpaper glue (available from most hardware stores), water and paper. Mix one part glue with three parts water, stirring well. Again, dip torn paper strips in the mixture before layering them onto the shape to be covered.

Recipe 3
Cold glue, water and paper. Mix two parts glue with one part lukewarm water, stirring well to form a paste. Dip torn paper strips in the mixture before layering them onto the shape.

For the best results, paper should be torn rather than cut, as this increases absorption. Make sure that each paper strip is well covered in the mixture before applying it to the shape. Layer the strips, allowing each layer to dry thoroughly before applying the next in order to ensure proper adhesion. If you find the smell of the papier-mâché intolerable, add some cinnamon to disguise the smell.

Finger paint

Both recipes work well. Although the boiled mixture will last somewhat longer, the second mixture can safely be made by an older child himself.

Recipe 1

- 3 cups of water
- 1 cup of cornflour
- a few drops of glycerine (for lustre)
- food colouring

Pour half of the water into a saucepan and bring to the boil. In a separate bowl, mix the cornflour with the rest of the water. Remove the saucepan from the heat, then add the cornflour mixture. Return to the heat, stirring continuously. Simmer for approximately one minute until the mixture is thick and translucent. Remove from the heat, then add one or two drops of glycerine. Divide the mixture and add different food colours.

Recipe 2

- 2 cups of cold water
- 2 cups of cake flour
- food colouring

Pour the water into a mixing bowl. Gradually add the flour, stirring continuously. Divide the mixture into smaller bowls and add different food colours.

Play goo

- 1 cup of grated Sunlight soap
- 2 litres of water

Combine the soap and water in a mixing bowl, then leave to stand for three days at room temperature. Stir occasionally.

Play dough

- 4 cups of cake flour
- 2 cups of salt
- 4 cups of warm water
- food colouring
- 4 tablespoons of cooking oil

Mix the dry ingredients. Add the food colouring to the water. (Textures such as grated coconut, or flavours such as peppermint or cocoa, which will add interest to the play dough can also be added now. Alternatively, different textures and flavours can be added to the finished product.) Combine all the ingredients in a saucepan, then stir over medium heat until the mixture is thick and smooth. Remove from the heat, allow to cool slightly, then knead until smooth and shiny. Store in an airtight container, keeping it in the fridge to extend its lifetime.

Warnings:
- Babies and children like to eat the clay, and although all the ingredients are edible, too much of it can make them sick. Children younger than five years should use the clay under supervision only.
- Adding colouring and flavouring will make the clay even more attractive to eat.
- If the clay has not been used for a while, carefully check for mould before allowing the child to use it again.

Additional reading

Barker, Kim, *Active Parenting* (series) (Cape Town: Maskew Miller Longman, 2001).
Brittz, Hettie, *Growing Kids with Character* (Vereeniging: Carpe Diem Publishers, 2007).
Cawood, Anne, *Children Need Boundaries:* Effective Discipline without Punishment (Welgemoed: Metz Press, 2007).
Davies, Kim, *The Handbook of Natural Baby & Childcare: Raising Your Baby and Child the Way Nature Intended from Birth to Age 5* (London: Hermes House, 2006).
Elias, Maurice J., Tobias, Steven E. and Friedlander, Brian S., *Emotionally Intelligent Parenting* (London: Hodder & Stoughton, 1999).
Eliot, Lise, *What's Going On In There?: How the Brain and Mind Develop in the First Five Years of Life* (New York: Bantam Books, 1999).
Faure, Megan and Richardson, Ann, *Baby Sense* (Welgemoed: Metz Press, 2002).
Faure, Megan and Richardson, Ann, *Sleep Sense* (Welgemoed: Metz Press, 2008).
Fourie, Margaret, *Talk!* (Welgemoed: Metz Press, 2007).
Gottman, John, *The Heart of Parenting: How to Raise a Self-Disciplined, Responsible, Socially Skilled Child* (London: Bloomsbury Publishing, 1997).
Leach, Penelope, *Your Baby and Child* (London: Penguin Books, 2003).
Lombard, Annemarie, *Sensory Intelligence: Why It Matters More than IQ and EQ* (Welgemoed: Metz Press, 2007).
Masi, Wendy S. and Leiderman, Roni Cohen, *Baby Play* (London: Time Life Books, 2001).
Masi, Wendy S. and Leiderman, Roni Cohen, *Toddler Play* (London: Time Life Books, 2001).
Osborne, Alison, *The Post-Baby Conversation: what new parents need to say to each other* (Welgemoed: Metz Press, 2008).
Pieterse, Martie, *Clever Talk* (South Africa: Metz Press, 1999).
Pieterse, Martie, *Slimkop/Smart Kid* (Welgemoed: Metz Press, 2008).
Richardson, Ann, *Toddler Sense* (Welgemoed: Metz Press, 2008).
Sunderland, Margot, *The Science of Parenting: Practical Guidance on Sleep, Crying, Play and Building Emotional Wellbeing for Life* (London: Penguin Books, 2006).
Woolfson, Richard C., *Bright Toddler* (London: Hamlyn, 2001).

www.babyhands.co.za
www.signlanguageforbaby.com
www.tinytalk.com.au

www.ingramcontent.com/pod-product-compliance
Ingram Content Group UK Ltd.
Pitfield, Milton Keynes, MK11 3LW, UK
UKHW050415240426
12048UKWH00021B/1529